PRAISE FOR ANNE MARIE'S FIRST BOOK,
BEYOND TERROR: ISLAM'S SLOW EROSION OF WESTERN DEMOCRACY

"*Beyond Terror* is one woman's story, but if Britain and any other nation is going to survive as a free society, this book should be taken as a template for what must be done, and for how everyone who values freedom must now become an activist—before it's too late."

Robert Spencer – Director, Jihad Watch

"This is a book about the threat to Britain and the free world from Islamic jihad and sharia, but it is also just as much about how the Left's hatred, authoritarianism, and cultural hegemony is strangling Britain from within, and leading to its very demise as a free nation."

Pamela Gellar – President, American Freedom Defense Initiative

"Anne Marie Waters is a courageous woman with integrity who stands on the strength of her convictions. Anne Marie is not afraid to speak the truth and will not be intimidated, bullied or silenced into submission for the views she holds. Anne Marie takes on the beast of political correctness and the hypocrisy of the Left, especially regarding Islam. She raises her voice for us all and gives us hope that sanity can prevail."

Kirralie Smith – Australian Conservatives

"The threat to the West goes beyond terror, and Ann Marie Waters' summary of this threat is incontrovertible. *Beyond Terror* outlines how, through a long march, and a paradoxical alliance with the Left, Islam has taken a hold of the inner workings and political leaders of the civilized West."

Jack Buckby – Author and Journalist

Printed in the United States of America
Original edition in 2020 in hardcover format
Paperback edition in 2024

ISBN: 978-0-9846938-6-3 (hardcover)
ISBN: 978-1-954102-22-4 (paperback)
ISBN: 978-1-954102-23-1 (ebook)
Library of Congress Control Number: 2020949456

Edited by Sarah Mayor
Cover design by Dragan Bilic
Interior design by Michael Grossman

Published by:
Laurania Press, an imprint of
SOMETHING OR OTHER PUBLISHING LLC
Brooklyn, Wisconsin 53521
For general inquiries: Info@SOOPLLC.com
For bulk orders: Orders@SOOPLLC.com

In
DEFENSE
of
DEMOCRACY

ANNE MARIE
WATERS

Contents

CONTENTS

PART 1:
THE TENETS
OF DEMOCRACY

Introduction

WRITING THIS BOOK CAME to mind several years ago. As a student, I worked as a doctor's PA. When I graduated, I left that job and the doctor I worked for brought me out for dinner before my departure date. We talked about various things, but one thing she said to me has stuck in my mind ever since. She asked, 'Why is democracy better?' and the seed was sown.

Why is democracy better? The first thing to ask is 'Better than what?' The obvious answer is *any other system except democracy*; that is what I believe and what I will argue in this book.

Democracy is the only system of government that takes into account the will of the people to determine who leads them and under what laws they will agree to live. All other systems consist of elitism – an unaccountable leader who, usually by fate of birth, is elevated to lead entire countries whether they have the aptitude for it or not. The country is run in accordance with the whim of an individual, an individual who may be benign or tyrannical; either way, the people have no say.

When an individual has elite power like this, the people are his slaves. Their lives are lived not in accordance with what is best for them and their families, but for the leader. The leader's will may, of course, be detrimental to the people, and herein lies the problem. The people are irrelevant and expendable; all that matters is one individual.

Collectivist philosophies like communism or fascism, consider the individual unimportant. What matters is the 'system' and maintaining it. This is why totalitarian societies always result in mass murder and oppression. In modern Western democracies, however, totalitarian societies are promoted, and democratic ones derided.

Following the Brexit referendum when the UK voted to leave the European Union, a severe anti-democracy propaganda session began in the British press. The elites believed that democracy had spoiled things for them, and that democracy itself was to blame.

Similar happened in the United States following the election of Donald Trump to the White House. The democrat elites and the press were equally appalled. 'How can this have happened?' they asked. 'Democracy' was the answer, and it was an answer that wasn't popular. Since his election, much of the US press, as well as the democrats, have tried every trick in the book, just as in the UK, to have the result ruled null and void. Democracy had brought about a result the elites didn't like. Hence, democracy had become a problem.

The Western world is, albeit slowly, becoming non-democratic. There is therefore a dire need for those of us who understand its superiority, to speak out loud and clear in its defence.

In this book, I will outline exactly why we must defend democracy, and how these democracies came about. They did not appear overnight; they were formed through bloodshed and tears. They have fought in defence of their democracies against external threats, and internal threats. As you will see, the history of humanity is a history of conflict between freedom and serfdom. Democracy is when freedom happens; anything else is serfdom.

I will explain how Europe became democratic, lost democracy, and then found it again. Following the Second World War, we had democracy once more, and it was strengthened. Now in 2020 it again is in peril. I will show how antidemocratic propaganda is used to persecute the only democracy in the Middle East: the tiny democratic state of Israel.

The United States is the world's leading democracy. Thanks to its constitution, many believe the USA will always be democratic, but this is simply untrue. America, as Europe, is facing an imminent danger, and it too must defend its constitution and republic, or it will be lost.

IN DEFENSE OF DEMOCRACY

Threats to democracy in 2020 are varied. Western democracies face destruction at the hands of China, Islam, the Far Left, and indeed Globalism. All these antidemocratic philosophies enjoy influence in the West today as never before because Western politicians and media have taken the side of tyranny. Our own journalists now campaign against our freedom, and our politicians dutifully do as they are told.

This is the story of our democracies. We must do all we can to ensure that our story does not come to a premature end.

In Defence of Democracy

THE WORD 'DEMOCRACY,' PROBABLY unsurprisingly, originates in ancient Greece. The Greek *'demos kratos'* translates as 'the strength of the people.' We will call it 'the will of the people.' It's a simple concept. It is the people of a country that should decide the fate of that country. Democracy does not, as in the case of totalitarianism, subject people to laws and regulations in which they have had no say in compiling.

There are certainly different ways in which the people can express their power, and there are different kinds of democracies, but for our purposes, we will stick with *representative democracy* – the most common method by which democratic countries are governed.

Representative democracy is familiar to us all. We elect people at election time, and they then make decisions. If we do not like their decisions, we can replace them with a new candidate at the next election. In other words, the theory is that it is the people who govern – not the state.

This is naturally imperfect, and like most ideologies, is more aspiration than reality. This does not lessen its importance though. All ideologies are just that: ideals. We cannot ever build an ideal society, but in striving for one, we take steps towards it, and those steps improve our society immeasurably; that's the case even if we never get it completely right. As we aspire to democracy (although we are unlikely to ever achieve it), the journey toward it is what gives us our rights.

So, democracy refers to the will of the people, but for millions of us to collectively decide upon who our leaders should be is obviously a practicable challenge. In fact, we do that bit quite well. Voting is the method we use, and it is only a method. To be clear, voting is not democracy, it is merely how we express it. Therefore, a country can hold an election, but if the whole thing is merely a series of going through the motions, it's not democracy. Furthermore, if people elect a tyrant, he is still a tyrant, even if elected.

Merely electing a dictator does not a democracy make. For example, leaders of Hamas in the West Bank were elected, but there has been no election since. There is no free speech, and no equality before the law; thus, elected or not, Hamas does not govern democratically. *The vote means very little when it means very little.* Similar situations exist in countries that hold elections in which the candidates are carefully chosen by the state, or there may be only one candidate. In this instance, voting is a show put on to create the impression of democracy.

The will of the people is, therefore, expressed at the ballot box via voting, and if things are done correctly, the person who gets the most support wins the contest, becoming the elected representative. If they perform well, they are likely to be re-elected, although that's certainly not a given. Those who perform poorly are likely to lose support, ie, votes. Those are the practicalities of it; that is how the people express their will. Our next question is: how do the people decide upon what their will is?

This is where free speech becomes crucial; it is the very principle that allows democracy to function on a political level. Let's be clear on what free speech is. Many seem to believe that free speech means we can say whatever we like, whenever we like, without consequence. Others believe they have had their free speech infringed upon if you happen to block them on Twitter. Of course, it is neither of these. It does not mean we can say what we like without consequence, it simply means we may say what we like without *legal* consequence – in other words, it is no concern of the State. However, what you say reveals who you are, and that has consequences. People may no longer want you around when they discover who you are, something they've discovered by what you said, and it is their right to decide who they spend time with. If you tell a friend how awful they are every time you see them, don't be surprised if they don't remain your friend! It won't be the concern of the police or the state, but it *is* the concern of your friend, and you will face the consequences of what you've said.

Freedom of speech is a civil right, a *political* right. It provides us with the ability to express our view on any matter, and to express it publicly so that others may hear it. A crucial point about free speech is that it refers not only to our right to speak, but our right to listen. Without the right to speak freely, and campaign freely, then we cannot communicate our views to the electorate, who then are denied the ability to agree and to vote accordingly.

When the people have heard all the candidates and their ideas freely, they then express their decision via voting at the ballot box, and the person with the most support wins. The next vital question is: why should the majority rule?

The first point to clarify about this is the essential difference between democracy and tyranny of the majority.

Democracy means the will of the people. It does not specify any further. It does not say male people, or white people, or heterosexual people, or people with dark hair. It is simply *the people*. All people have the right to express their will, and all the people retain those rights after they have done so. If, for example, a candidate has based his or her campaign on removing the rights of a minority – homosexuals, for instance – and people vote affirmatively and homosexuals lose their rights, this is an example of majority tyranny. In democracy, the homosexual retains his or her essential rights, because they are also 'the people.'

Like democracy itself, the will of the majority (not the tyranny of the majority) determines policy simply because it is the fairest way. How else would we decide who comes to power if not by the will of the majority? Should a minority rule over the majority? *(It's certainly very popular, but I would suggest that it is as immoral as it is common.)* People have been domi-nated by unaccountable power throughout history, as they are today in all corners of the world – and it's immoral. The reason? Liberty. The removal of a person's democratic rights is the removal of their ability to live their lives in relative freedom, to have a say in the rules that govern them, and to demand a change in those laws by exercising the voting power to remove the leaders who enacted them.

Democracy allows us to have a say in our lives. It empowers us. It has a profound effect on our sense of personal strength and autonomy, and it helps to ensure our liberties. It is for this reason that those in power, such as in the European Union for example, are often not that keen on elections! Those who oppose democracy do so because they believe the majority is uneducated or does not understand the issues correctly. Not only is this extraordinary snobbery (snobbery is a major anti-democratic driver in society), but it creates a stark class division and a stark elitism. The elites 'know best' and will decide how things are done. For example, if their decisions have a detrimental effect on low-income people, that doesn't concern them because the elite aren't low income. Furthermore, there's nothing the low-income people can do about it – at least not without democracy.

Democracy is also inescapably linked to liberty; a government may take away our liberties for their own benefit, and without democracy, we cannot stop them. In short, the reason you have the freedoms you have is because you have the vote you have.

'Freedom' is a word used often, but rarely explained or discussed in any great detail. The dictionary offers this: 'the power or right to act, speak, or think as one wants' and 'the state of not being imprisoned or enslaved.' These are objective positions, and freedom, therefore, has an objective meaning. If you value your freedom, you will value democracy because this is the vessel in which you retain your freedom. Sadly (and this is how dictators rise), not everyone wants to be free.

Freedom comes with responsibility, and that is unattractive to many. On the left wing of politics, freedom is unpopular, and it is true that many millions of people will happily forfeit their freedom in return for a promised 'safety' that can never be delivered. No government can truly keep us safe, as hazards are all around us – that's life. But they can promise us that they will do so, and can be convincing. This concept was perfectly illustrated with the outbreak of coronavirus.

People – the entire Western world, in fact – handed over our every liberty to the government to be kept safe from a virus.

This kind of State dependence requires a great deal of trust in our government, something many people find near impossible to do. We don't necessarily believe all of our governments are nefarious. Incompetence may be an issue, or more importantly, a government often decides what is best; their 'best' is usually what's best *for them*, and may not be what's best *for you*.

That's where freedom comes in; your right to decide how to live your life, restricted only by the right of others to do the same. We do not have the 'freedom' to remove the freedoms of others, nor to infringe upon them.

America has phrased this perfectly: 'Life, Liberty and the pursuit of Happiness.' It is the latter part of this statement that is subjective, and therefore, only personal liberty can provide it. The fact is that we are all made 'happy' by something different. We are all individuals and enjoy different things. Some of us will be made happy or content by a successful career, others in raising a healthy family, others will be happy to be fully engaged in public life, while others want to be left alone. Some want to marry, some don't. We all have our own preferred way of making our way through life, and only liberty allows it. We can be assured of our liberty if we have a say in our governance. That's the true importance of democracy.

It is because of this that I argue very clearly – democracy is not just 'different' from totalitarianism or tyranny, it is *better*. It is superior. It is the system that allows people to be free, and therefore happy. It is the most moral system. To impose unhappiness upon people in this one and only life they will ever have, is a deeply immoral act.

In short, for the reasons just outlined, and despite its shortcomings, democracy is morally superior to any other system of government. Or, to put it as the great Winston Churchill did, 'Democracy is the worst form of government, except for all the others.'

So where did it all come from? How did it get started? That's not an easy question to answer, as some kind of citizen participation has been practiced in various parts of the world for eons. Despite that, the origins of democracy trace back to ancient Greece, so that is where we will begin.

In 600 BC, the city state of Athens (together with its immediate surroundings known as Attica) developed a system that would become known as 'democracy.' It wasn't quite as we know it today, but ancient Greece is still regarded by many as the world's first known democratic state.

Athenian democracy was based upon participation and legislation via executive bills, much like it is today. Prior to that, Athens had been ruled by a system of magistrates, usually aristocrats. These magistrates were known as 'archons' and it was, for the most part, they themselves who first promoted democratic notions. One such archon, Solon, is credited by many as the creator (or inventor) of democracy.

While chief archon, Solon issued a decree that all citizens were to participate in the governing of Athens. He said that citizens were now free – and welcome – to attend and take part in meetings of an assembly that would be comprised of 400 members from across Athens. It was open to every male citizen who had completed military training, which comprised anywhere between 30,000 and 60,000 men, or about 10–20% of the population.

Written law, to be enforced only by courts, was introduced by another archon, Draco. To this day, these systems are still in place throughout the world.

Similar to the rest of Europe, the history of democracy in Greece is one of 'back and forth.' Wars were fought for centuries between those who wanted the will of the people, and those who preferred their own unaccountable rule.

Today, Greece is a democracy, albeit one within the European Union. Its current structure was put in place in 1975, following the overthrow of a military junta two years earlier, which had ruled since 1969.

In 1981, Greece joined the 'European Community' – now the 'European Union.' In the 2010s, the unelected 'European Commission' blackmailed Greece, (which, at the time, was suffering dire economic conditions), paying billions of euros in return for the implementation of their policies in Athens. It worked. The EU had control of Greece, irrespective of how its people decided to vote. EU-imposed austerity policies in Greece officially lasted eight years, but even today, unelected EU chiefs continue to make policy demands of the Greek government.

The non-democratic ideologies of the world are largely similar. Communism, socialism, and fascism are different, yes, but not by a great deal. All are authoritarian and *that* is the fundamental aspect that can never be compatible with the aspiration to democracy. Let's look at these (and others) in more detail.

COMMUNISM

Communism essentially refers to collective ownership. The means of production are owned by a single party state.

Communists seek a classless society. The ideology was promoted by Karl Marx in his *Communist Manifesto,* in which he argued that workers would inevitably rise up and seize control from the property-owning *bourgeoisie.*

Marx believed that the transformation of capitalism to communism would happen in two stages. In the first phase, the working class would take control of the economy and government, but would still have to pay people based on hours worked, etc. Communism proper would be the second phase, no government would be involved at all. The mantra 'from each according to his ability, to each according to his need' is the ideal.

Sadly, for communists, it can only remain an ideal because it is entirely impossible in practice. If guided by such a mantra, the first question is: how would we know what someone's ability is? How would we know what their needs are? How can we then expect 'according to ability' and give 'according to need'? It depends on 100% agreement, 100% cooperation, and 100% honesty. Anyone with common sense knows that isn't going to happen. Furthermore, how can a society exist with no leadership? It can't; it is entirely chaotic. In practice, of course, communism operates nothing like this. That ideal is unreachable, and while most ideals are, the road to achieving communism is far darker than the road to democracy.

We know this from history, and we know it from current-day affairs.

By far, the most powerful communist country in the world is China (see 'Threats to Democracy'). China is currently the second largest economy in the world, behind the United States. The four largest banks in the world are now Chinese banks, and that country produces vast amounts of products – Western countries are swamped with 'Made in China' products. But it wasn't until China participated in capitalist practices that it became a powerhouse. China was happy to enter the world of global trade – and was more than welcomed to do so. But, as was naively expected, it did not discover democracy as an accompaniment to its newfound capitalism.

As you might expect, China is not run 'by the people' and the means of production are owned by the unelected Chinese Communist Party; they live in luxury while millions of Chinese still live in abject poverty (so much for 'to each according to need').

Communism needs full agreement; everyone must go along with it for the ideal to be reached. As previously mentioned, that can't happen (human nature won't allow it), but regardless, it is enforced. If you don't agree, you'll be forced to agree. That is where communism becomes totalitarianism. There is no political accountability, no freedom of speech (one can't criticize the system), and individuals are dispensable. All that matters is the collective.

Therefore, individual life is cheap, and the Chinese government makes sure its people know it. It was equally cheap in Soviet Russia, where gulags and re-education camps were built for dissenters, neighbours spied on each other, and queues of desperate people filled the streets, seeking basic necessities. Communism is advertised as utopia; the reality is closer to misery.

SOCIALISM

Socialism and communism are closely linked; indeed, Karl Marx used the two words interchangeably. For Marx, socialism was the first phase of the transition (from capitalism to communism), while the second phase was pure communism. Socialism is generally seen as less extreme and more pragmatic than communism. For example, most Western societies cater to both socialist and capitalist economic systems. In European countries, a healthy welfare state is enjoyed by most citizens, as is universal healthcare and education. Policing, fire service, etc., are all paid for and used collectively. However, what products are available, and how much we have to spend on them, is subject to market conditions.

Like communism, socialism opposes capitalism, and like communism, it simply does not work in practice. Capitalism works because of incentivisation, creativity, and individual entrepreneurship. People will not be motivated if there is no reward; that is the essence of the failure of communist and socialist economics. It also prevents a society from getting the most out of its resources. It is easier for people to waste something if they don't feel an infinity to it; in other words, if it isn't theirs.

Collective ownership of this kind gives power to the State, not to the people. It is the State that decides the value of things rather than the market. Life in a communist or socialist society is strictly regulated and controlled, and the ingenuity of individuals is crushed. As many democrats and freedom fighters realise, socialism and authoritarianism go hand in hand. Our ability to live our lives freely, or to pursue the American ideal of 'happiness,' is not only hampered, but erased by a controlling State.

Collectivism of this sort is based very much on an unrealistically positive view of the world. In *Modern Political Ideologies*, Andrew Vincent writes of socialism:

> 'Socialists usually have an optimistic developmental view of human beings; they tend to embrace, to some degree, a perfectibility thesis.'

While optimism is a positive outlook, it will lead to endless disappointment if not mixed with a healthy dose of reality.

15

FASCISM

Fascism is not as distinguishable from communism and socialism as left-wingers would like to pretend. A product of the 20th century, fascism flowered in Europe with the rise of Hitler in Germany and Mussolini in Italy. It derives from the Latin word 'fasces,' meaning bundles of rods bound together in a symbol of strength in unity. Once again, collectivism is evident. There are links with socialism throughout history, and Mussolini (Italy's notorious fascist dictator), began his political life as a socialist. Hitler's party was a national socialist party.

Fascism shares several characteristics with communism and socialism. It is authoritarian, will not tolerate political opposition, opposes individual freedoms, and crushes all liberalism. It believes in the rule of the elites, and while communism pretends not to agree, in practice, communism's leaders are very 'elite' indeed. To take a simplistic view, the distinction can be made with reference to the militaristic nationalism of fascism.

Economically, there are further distinctions. While communism and socialism call for collective ownership of the means of production, fascism's primary economic goal is autarky – complete self-sufficiency. However, most economists believe that fascism has no defined economic system, and that each fascist State works differently. Mussolini, for instance, believed in an economic system where the State directed economic production and the allocation of resources.

Hitler was determined to improve the economic situation of Germany, as he knew this was his path to maintaining power. However, he supported and sought autarky as the ultimate goal. For example, he established tariffs on imports in a protectionist move. The Mises Institute, (an organisation that promotes individuality) and the Austrian School of Economics described Hitler's early economic policies as follows:

He suspended the gold standard, embarked on huge public-works programs like autobahns, protected industry from foreign competition, expanded credit, instituted jobs programs, bullied the private sector on prices and production decisions, vastly expanded the military, enforced capital controls, instituted family planning, penalized smoking, brought about national healthcare and unemployment insurance, imposed education standards, and eventually ran huge deficits. The Nazi interventionist program was essential to the regime's rejection of the market economy and its embrace of socialism in one country.

Hitler's economics cannot be easily pigeonholed, lending credence to the notion that fascism itself does not come with an economic policy, but is a political philosophy only.

CAPITALISM

I'm adding capitalism here, not to pretend it is similar to the systems above, but merely to briefly examine how and why it goes hand in hand with democracy. Capitalism can be subject to legitimate criticisms. Many would argue that unfettered (or unregulated) capitalism can lead to a society with little to no workers' rights, no environmental protections, and no concern for the social fallout of capitalist decisions. In its purest form, it is about profit. It centres around the individual and the rights of individuals to create a product, sell it, and keep the proceeds (subject to taxation, of course!).

It works through incentivism; the more reward a person receives, the more motivated they are. The capitalist philosophy is simply that individuals will prioritise themselves, and work for themselves for their own benefit, and this will drive society.

Capitalism allows for private ownership; the means of production are owned by individuals and not by the State. This ownership is incredibly important if we are to maintain individual powers. A person is far less powerful if dependent upon the State for their very being: food, clothing, shelter. If we depend on the State for these things, then the State controls us. This is the totalitarian element of collectivism laid bare.

Capitalism, however, goes hand in hand with personal freedom and with individuals owning their own property and money; they do not require State intervention for their survival. Property ownership gives power to the individual, wealth gives power to the individual, our liberty to create, sell, and trade is a fundamental freedom – one that capitalism promotes.

Capitalism runs a market-led economy, driven by consumer choice. The production of goods is based upon supply and demand, and prices are determined similarly. (Authoritarian economic systems, on the other hand, tend to drive the economy centrally.) The capitalist idea is that consumer choice drives standards up as firms compete for customers and are incentivized to improve their product or cut prices (or both). Furthermore, there is less waste in capitalist societies because when an economy is profit-driven, those who seek the profit will fight waste.

While many will call capitalism exploitative or conscience-free, this is only true if there are no regulations. The idea that all rich people have no conscience (no regard for the environment or workers' rights), is entirely unfair and deliberately attempts to portray capitalism and capitalists as soulless, lacking concern for wider society. This kind of imagery and rhetoric is usually pushed by those of a left-wing bent. Some argue that capitalism and democracy are incompatible, given that democracy provides equality of citizenship, while capitalism produces economic inequality. This is a deeply flawed argument. Capitalism does not produce anything; it is an idea about the means of production, the reward for production, and the incentivisation for production. Unequal wealth is created by unequal contribution. Poverty may cause this unequal contribution, or poor education systems, or class snobbery, but capitalism itself is not to blame. Those other issues could, and would, be tackled by a democratic government in the interests of its people, enabling everyone with the opportunity to compete in a capitalist economy.

Overall – and probably the most important point to make – is that capitalism *works*. All the world's first-world countries are both democratic and capitalist; the fact that they are the world's richest countries is not a coincidence. There are different kinds of capitalism, and none of these systems are un-regulated, (ie, there is legislation for workers' rights and environmental protections), but the fundamentals are there, and they are the same as the fundamentals of democracy: individual freedom and the 'ownership' of a nation by its people, not by its government.

In Defence of Free Speech

WHEN I WAS A student, I taught what I was taught. I studied journalism in Nottingham, a city in the English East Midlands, for three years. During that time, I earned extra cash teaching journalism to children in primary schools across the Midlands region.

The current generation of university students is known (not affectionately) as the 'snowflake' generation, partly due to a 'feelings-before-facts' political correctness that reigns supreme over academia (more on this later). The snowflake generation is, therefore, not known to be crazy about free speech; it may hurt someone's feelings. This did not happen overnight. When I was at university (approximately 20 years ago), free speech wasn't shouted from the rooftops as a virtue. Still, I have always been a fan, for the simple reasons I will outline below.

Having to teach a serious subject to young children presented a challenge. I wanted the children to enjoy the experience, but I also wanted them to take something important away from it. I was particularly interested in free speech and thought of ways to include this in my lessons, somehow making it fun, as well. I had the perfect idea.

The university agreed to loan me television equipment to do the job. I would take the camera to the school, create a TV news show with the kids as writers, guests, and anchors. Then, I would film the show and play it back for the class to watch. The kids loved it – it was a huge success.

So, how did I teach them about free speech? I used our 'pre-broadcast editorial meeting.'

I started with what I explained as *the basics*. What is the point of the news? It is to inform people of the current goings-on in politics, culture, and society. The journalist's job is to go out and find what's happening, then report it back to the reading (or viewing) public. Their primary purpose is communication and connection, but they also fill an arm of the political process in terms of facilitating communication between political candidates and the electorate.

They got that. Now, on to free speech. How do we know who is allowed to write what?

I gave the kids pieces of paper with the words 'good idea,' 'bad idea,' and one with 'best idea' written on them. (The subjectivity of good vs bad idea was not relevant to the point). I then split the kids into two groups, making sure that the holder of 'best idea' was in the group I wanted. I told one side they could express their idea, and the other side that they could not. On the side that couldn't speak was, of course, the 'best idea,' but we never heard it since *that* person wasn't allowed to speak.

They got that as well. Immediately, free speech meant something to them, and I hope it still does today.

Following our free speech talk, we'd get on with the fun part!

This is a simplistic way to describe a fundamental facet of free speech, and one that can be defended on several grounds.

How can we progress in the best way if some people are not permitted to speak? How can we hold free and fair elections if certain candidates are not allowed to speak? Just think what (and who) we might be missing out on!

The reason for opposition to free speech is that it allows for the expansion of ideas an opposing individual isn't fond of. This is the great fear of democracy – that it could bring the 'wrong' results. If people are able to speak freely, then they could persuade others, and that might result in political change. But, that's the *entire point*. We must be able to make political change. This change will not always be for the better, and when we err, free speech allows us to put it right again. In fact, it is democracy that allows us to put it right again, but democracy cannot exist without free speech.

IN DEFENSE OF DEMOCRACY

I mentioned that the media is the facilitator between politicians and the people. Indeed, this is true. The media, therefore, fulfils a vital element of the democratic process. Given its significance, we might expect the media to be honest, but as we know, that isn't always the case.

However, the relationship with politics is the lifeblood of democracy. It is open to corruption (and is corrupt), and it has far too much influence on the decisions made by politicians who often prioritise headlines over constituents. That aside, it is uncontroversial to argue that in a democracy, politicians are elected largely based upon what the media has reported about them. This results in a relationship of interdependence, one that is a threat to democracy itself.

How so? Because the press can lie, misrepresent, and favour its own bias. It also has advertisers to think of, and the potential for political fallout. For example, a paper (or TV, radio, or other media) may object to the political proposals of a candidate, choosing to misrepresent them. Like our children in school, some people are, therefore, prevented from speaking because their words are wrongly reported. Consequently, the voter does not have the true facts in front of them to assist their decision in terms of for whom to cast their vote.

Freedom of the press is a more complex matter than it initially appears. Yes, it is fundamental to democracy that the press is free. The reason for this is to provide the press with the ability to hold the powerful to account, and to report whatever they find about any person, so that the public is fully informed.

Sadly, as human nature is involved, the media is corruptible. As mentioned, journalists have political opinions and this shows in journalism, now as never before. The concept of unbiased journalism is a thing of the past.

Few have experienced the wrath of the mainstream press like those who have spoken out against government policies; particularly those surrounding immigration, Islam, or both. It is now widely understood across British society that a non-conforming opinion on these topics will trigger the press to issue reports that are entirely inaccurate, defamatory, and which may well have the effect of placing the targeted person in danger.

It is a true statement: the British press will destroy lives without a moment's consideration. Is this free speech? Let's examine it.

The best place to start is with myself and my own history with the press. Throughout my political career, my core beliefs have remained solid. I began in the mainstream party on the left of British politics, the Labour Party. I was a trade union rep; I worked in the National Health Service, and belonged to a campaign group dedicated to its preservation. I was an outspoken campaigner against rape and sexual abuse, and indeed, the abuses of women and girls. I supported civil liberties, the empowerment of the citizen against the State, and workers' rights to a decent wage. Most of these tenets would be associated with left-wing politics, and I still believe in all of them. I also, however, believe in controlled and minimal migration (particularly between countries with vastly different cultures). I believe in patriotism and nation-state democracy. I believe in the right of all – including white Europeans – to respect and integrity in relation to skin colour, culture, ethnicity, and homeland.

I also believe in secularism, having fought the excesses of religion much of my adult life (see 'In Defence of Secularism' below). I have served on the governing board of the UK's largest secularism campaign group, the National Secular Society. I supported (and still support) secular societies because they are in tune with my fundamental, overriding, and primary belief in the liberty of the individual.

I have spoken openly and honestly about my beliefs since I first began public speaking or writing. I have never wavered. It's true that some of my beliefs have changed; I'm no longer as naïve or idealistic as in my youth and I now realize that one can only do their best for their community. Saving the world isn't an option. But this aside, my core beliefs have remained. These beliefs are neither racist, nor hateful, nor extreme. But that is not the view of the press.

My battle with the lies of the press began during the leadership contest for the UK Independence Party (UKIP). *The Telegraph*, the largest conservative newspaper in the UK, labelled me 'neo-fascist' in one of its headlines. This was just the start. It was written by a fellow Ukipper who, at that point, I had never met. But there it was. I was denounced as a neo-fascist and there was nothing I could do about it. The charges were made even though I have never so much as hinted at sympathy with fascism; indeed, quite the opposite.

The manifesto I produced for the UKIP leadership didn't resemble fascism in any way. It was an accurate reflection of my true belief in the power of the citizen against the State. It was a call for liberty, democracy, and truth. It was a call for the government to put its own people first, to carry out its moral duties towards its electorate, and above all, to be accountable to the people of Britain. This is not fascism. It is nowhere close to fascism, but I was not allowed to reply. *The Telegraph* affixed me with a label and made no attempt to approach me to ask me about that label.

This scenario constantly repeats itself. *The Sun* published an article entitled 'Who is Anne Marie Waters?' and, once again, I wasn't included in the formation of that article. They asked a question without allowing me to answer. *The Irish Times* did similarly; they asked who I was but made no attempt to get an answer from me.

Nick Cohen, in *The Guardian*, denounced me as a 'bigot.' I've met and spoken with Cohen on several occasions. He knows my history and the work I've done, but because I joined UKIP, I was suddenly someone else – someone he could simply denounce without justification.

Finally, one more example. Scotland's *Daily Record* went even further and suggested that I was running some kind of military outfit. The article was the very definition of defamation and every trick in the book was used. Stephen Stewart wrote: 'We can reveal that far-right extremist group "For Britain" has deployed an activist in Scotland to try to develop links among serving and retired forces personnel.'

Note the use of language like 'deployed,' which suggests military-like campaigning. Furthermore, pictures of me were interspersed with pictures of people from groups like Combat 18 (an avowed neo-Nazi group) and included a photo of one such activist standing in front of a swastika flag holding a machine gun. Also included was a photo of a 'white supremacist' who had been jailed for eight years.

This is both hugely clever and entirely rotten. Pictures speak a thousand words and all anyone had to do was glance over this article to be left with the impression that I am in the same league as 'Combat 18' or 'white supremacists.'

I said the article was the definition of defamation; it would be if I had, at least, the same rights as other people. The problem for me is that I have been denounced as far-right, and when that happens it releases a domino effect.

'Journalism' in the UK works like this: one newspaper gives you a certain label, with no right to reply, and the article including that label goes on to Wikipedia. 'Hope Not Hate,' a group which exists to create racists and neo-Nazis in order to give themselves an enemy and keep the funds coming, will be asked their view of me (I will not be asked), and that all goes on Wiki for all to see.

Then another 'journalist' comes along. What does their 'research' consist of? Wikipedia. They pick up on the last article that called me a Nazi/fascist/far-right/racist and they repeat it. That article then goes on Wikipedia for the next 'journalist' to pick up the baton.

I have no ability to change or challenge Wikipedia. I have no ability to change or challenge the articles contained within it. I am stuck on the outside looking in at people who are calling me all the shocking names imaginable. I am not allowed inside to respond to those accusations. I must stand there silently and watch while my reputation is torn to shreds, without an opportunity to defend myself.

That is what passes for 'journalism' in Britain, but is it a manifestation of free speech?

No, it is not. It is an abuse of free speech. Let's be clear what free speech is.

Free speech is something that is often widely (and wildly) misunderstood. First, it is a political right, a civil right, and its purpose is to rein in the power of the powerful. Its role in democracy is to allow those who wish to step forward and present criticisms of government policy and put forward opposing proposals, to do so. Combined with the other integral civil right, freedom of association, it allows citizens to form groups and discuss specific issues publicly (or privately). It allows citizens to form their own political parties and put their ideas to the electorate. That is its importance and its significance. It means, bluntly, that we can say what we like, express our opinion, and it is of no concern whatsoever to the State. In fact, the only interest the State (ie, the police) should have in free speech is to *protect it.* Again however, in Britain today, police are more concerned with shutting down free speech than with protecting it.

A further example from my own experiences: I stood in a parliamentary by-election in 2017. Parliament is the most senior legislature in the United Kingdom and elections to it are fairly significant news. The election was for a parliamentary seat in the south of London, Lewisham East.

During the campaign, local activists organized a single hustings event, and, to their credit, I was invited. In discussions with the organiser, he told me people had a right to hear from me, and I agreed to attend. On the night of the event, left-wing troublemakers gathered around the entrance to the building, preventing access. They shouted that I was not to take part in their democracy.

My security team had forewarned the police that such an occurrence was likely, but the police paid no heed. Only when the crowds were so large that people could not make their way into the venue, did they attempt to take any action. The action they took was to *tell me to stay away.* My security team was told by venue police that the event was to be cancelled, but this was not entirely true. Having been told to stay away because the evening was called off, I saw on social media that it was, in fact, under way. So, I told the police I was going to attend; it was at that point that they actually cancelled it, but only after every other candidate had spoken.

Left-wing activists disrupted a parliamentary hustings with the ever-present threat of violence, and instead of dispersing the crowd and protecting my right to speak, the police sided with the protestors and got rid of me.

The press, who are usually keen to give me all the wrong headlines, weren't even slightly concerned about this incident. I was a parliamentary candidate prevented from attending a hustings by violent left-wing mobs, backed up by the police, and the press saw nothing of interest to report. It is entirely obvious that if I were a left-wing candidate silenced by a right-wing mob (with the assistance of the police), it would have made international headlines.

Free speech is a tricky concept and it is easy to misunderstand. Freedom of the press is part of it, but that, in itself, is complex. If we compare countries, China, for instance, the press there is totally controlled by the communist State. Therefore, the press only prints things that do not threaten the political status quo. The UK is now remarkably similar – journalists protect the status quo at the expense of potential newcomers. The press is, essentially, an arm of the two-party State. This is not written down anywhere, it's not 'official,' but it is the reality.

UK politics is dominated by two major parties (not quite as dominated as America, but dominated, nonetheless – for now) and the press quite likes it this way. Power shifts between Labour and the Conservatives; back and forward, back and forward.

In China, there is a ruling elite that engineers life. Likewise, in the UK, there is a ruling elite that engineers life, and they can be found drinking in the wine bars of Westminster. MPs spend a great deal of time and energy on courting the press, eating, and drinking together. MPs are likely to spend as much time, if not more, in the company of journalists than in that of their own constituents. It is a tight-knit affair and the journalism elites (such as the BBC) know the MPs well. The role of the press in this scenario is to keep the two-party State alive and well, and for doing so, they'll be granted access to politics that independent journalists, for example, may well be denied.

How does the press keep the powerful in power? By denouncing all challengers to this power. They do this ostensibly by using their free speech, but as stated, this is not free speech at all; it's an *abuse of it*. Real free speech would be to give fair coverage to challengers and allow the democratic process to take place, for the electorate to hear the truth and vote based upon it.

Over the last few decades, serious challengers to the Westminster elite have been utterly shredded by the press. UKIP is one example. From the outset, UKIP was described as 'racist' and 'fascist' simply because it campaigned to leave the European Union. It's true that UKIP eventually broke through to some extent, but only after it had worked tirelessly to fend off the accusations levelled at it by the press. Producing a manifesto and allowing the people to decide was not acceptable to the press; it had to smear and slander in order to keep UKIP at bay and maintain Labour/Tory control of the House of Commons.

This in no way can be described as genuine democracy. It also raises serious questions about free speech; who decides what should be heard and what should not? In truth, unelected journalists decide this, and they do so in their own interests – both political and financial.

Journalists need to make a living and will, therefore, write what editors want them to write. If an editor is pro-Labour, then a journalist must be pro-Labour (if they want to work for that editor). Left-wing publications will hire only left-wing journalists who will report with the expected slant, denouncing all of those who are not left-wing. Facts are irrelevant; if a person does not adhere to the left's tenets, they become whatever the journalist wants them to be, and the victim is left without any ability to respond.

The way the press presents information can also be incredibly biased – and incredibly dishonest. A journalist can string sentences together to say something completely different than what was meant by the speaker or author. They often leave out lines altogether, completely decontextualizing what was said. There is very little one can do about this because the speaker/author may have said the sentence, but said it very differently than is presented. These practices are common, but what is becoming more common is outright lying by the press about right-wing figures.

In effect, then, the media decides who shall be heard and who shall not be heard. Much of the media is left-wing, so the consequences are obvious. But it isn't solely the mainstream press that is to blame for this disruption of democracy and free speech; social media is every bit as guilty.

The main giants of social media are Facebook, Twitter, and YouTube. All three have implanted themselves into the heart of political campaigning. US President Donald Trump famously used Twitter with enormous effect in campaigning for the White House – much to the disgust of the Silicon Valley bigshots. Following the election of Donald Trump in 2016, Google (the world's largest search engine and owner of YouTube) executives and staff gathered to console one another. In a leaked video, Google co-founder Sergey Brin revealed he was feeling 'sad' about the election result, and added, 'As an immigrant and a refugee, I certainly find this election deeply offensive.'

He found the voice of the American public 'deeply offensive' because it did not go his way. This man controls Google, and Google controls exactly what you find when you carry out a search. Even so, he had no problem at all showing his political bias for all the world to see.

Trump has accused Google of 'rigging' their search results against him. He wrote on Twitter:

'Google search results for "Trump News" shows only the viewing/reporting of fake news media. In other words, they have it RIGGED.'

Google furiously denied this, but their political bias can't be so easily side-stepped.

Twitter is yet another social media giant which sees no particular issue in promoting some politics while banning others. I have been removed from Twitter for accurately referring to members of Britain's notorious rape gangs as 'Muslim' (because they are). Now, people can tweet lies and misrepresentations about me to their hearts' content, and there is nothing I can do to answer back, because I have been banned by Twitter.

While I remain banned, Twitter allows tweets that promote female genital mutilation (this is just one example). FGM is a criminal offence in many countries, particularly in the West, but nonetheless, Twitter allowed the following tweet to be published:

> *'My daughters have also undergone khafz [FGM], and they're growing up as perfectly as other children of their age. As a mother, I can never do anything to harm them' says Arwa Sohangpurwala, Chartered Accountant, Kolkata.*

Twitter has also banned Tommy Robinson and a host of others who are pro-nationalism, anti-Islam, or anti–mass migration. It is no great leap to figure out that Twitter is also keen on political bias.

Facebook is more of the same. Its CEO, Mark Zuckerberg, was famously recorded discussing censorship with German Chancellor Angela Merkel. Zuckerberg assured the Chancellor that he was 'working on' removing so-called 'hate' posts from its platform. 'Hate' was, in reality, criticism of Merkel's open-border policy which had brought a wave of crime and terrorism to the country.

Facebook has closed accounts of people merely for typing the name 'Tommy Robinson,' dishing out suspensions for those who shared a video of a post promoting my own important work. (My thought at the time was 'look how important we are.')

Obvious political bias has convinced many politically aware people that the mainstream press cannot be trusted. Criticisms of the 'MSM' (mainstream media) are now widespread and commonplace, as is distrust of the mainstream social media. Reporters have been caught out engaging in flagrant misreporting, and nobody has brought this to public attention quite like Donald Trump.

Trump coined the phrase 'fake news' and most people now associate that phrase with a dishonest press. This is both a positive and negative development. Positive because distrust of a press that has shown itself as dishonest is obviously a good thing; the public is paying attention. To look at it from a negative viewpoint, however, we are currently stuck (for the time being) with a dishonest mainstream media that, despite the growing distrust, impacts the thinking of millions of people.

The press is a threat to free speech because it abuses it to lie and mislead, thus distorting the process of democracy. Likewise, it engineers (or tries to engineer) elections according to its own politics. While this is nothing new, 24-hour TV news, along with the advancement of the internet, has changed the level of exposure people have to the MSM. I'd argue that press bias is a bigger threat than ever; on the flip side, more people are aware of it than ever.

The law does little to tackle press bias. Why would legislators force newspapers to stop smearing their opponents? I am not suggesting a conspiracy between politics and press, but some things don't need to be written down or spoken about, they just 'are.' The cosy relationship between mainstream politicians and journalists keeps them all at the top of the heap, maintaining their position as the elite so they instinctively want to keep things that way. This comes at the expense of democracy and the best interests of the voting public – and that's the problem.

Instead of tackling press bias, one could argue that the law, in fact, aids it. This is particularly true of so-called 'hate speech' laws.

Under Tony Blair, the British Labour Government introduced (at the behest of many Islamic 'community leaders') the Racial and Religious Hatred Act of 2006 (RRHA). This piece of legislation is an apt demonstration of how our laws have infringed upon our speech, and with extraordinarily little protest.

RRHA introduced something entirely staggering to UK law; it gave power to police or bystanders to increase a person's prison sentence based purely on their opinion as to what was taking place. It has introduced guilt-by-opinion, leading police into a totalitarian mindset; our policing has changed drastically.

The legislation altered the Public Order Act of 1986 and controversially states:

Section 29A
- Meaning of 'religious hatred'
- In this Part 'religious hatred' means hatred against a group of persons defined by reference to religious belief or lack of religious belief.

Section 29B:
- (1) A person who uses threatening words or behaviour, or displays any written material which is threatening, is guilty of an offence if he intends thereby to stir up religious hatred.

No definition of 'hatred' is offered. When one looks at the interpretation of this legislation, particularly by the Crown Prosecution Service (CPS, the public body responsible for prosecuting criminal offences in the UK) and the Metropolitan Police (the police service of London, the largest in the UK), it is then that one realises the harrowing effect on free speech. It must be remembered that it isn't only those who are accused of a crime (or taken before the courts) who are affected by this. It is the example set by individual cases that is responsible for the wider damage. The courts and the police, by prosecuting or arresting, send a message to broad society that we are no longer free to say controversial things; they will decide what constitutes 'controversial.' Even if this message is vague and misunderstood, as is so often the case, the damage is done because the message to the public has been sent, and self-censorship will be the outcome.

Here is the CPS's take on racial and religious hatred:

The CPS uses definitions agreed with the National Police Chiefs' Council to identify racist or religious incidents/crimes and to monitor the decisions and outcomes:

'Any incident/crime which is perceived by the victim or any other person to be motivated by hostility or prejudice based on a person's race or perceived race'

or

'Any incident/crime which is perceived by the victim or any other person to be motivated by a hostility or prejudice based on a person's religion or perceived religion.'

Flagging is a subjective question. Flagging a case puts the CPS on notice that someone at some stage has perceived the incident that gave rise to the case had such an element of racial or religious hostility or prejudice to it. For a conviction to receive enhanced sentencing in court the police need to provide sufficient evidence to prove the hostility element, however this is not required for flagging purposes.

Therefore, whilst not all flagged cases will result in specific racially or religiously aggravated charges or an application for an uplift of sentence under s145 of the Criminal Justice Act 2003, they should still be flagged on CMS.

It is not CPS policy to remove a flag in the absence of sufficient evidence to support a sentence uplift.

Let's go through this in some detail.

'Hate' is identified as an aggravating factor. I don't find the word 'facto' in this context, only in the phrase 'de facto' by CPS and police. If a bystander merely says that *they* believe the incident was prompted by religious hatred, it's accepted. While this is subject to reasonableness, there is nothing at all to prevent a police officer (for example) from testifying that the incident (whatever that incident may have been) was caused partly due to religious hatred. Potentially, no further evidence needs to be considered. But it is the 'flagging' element that should ring alarms most loudly.

To 'flag' an incident as motivated by religious hatred is simply to make a note of it, even when no crime has been identified. The consequence of this? A database has been created containing the details of people who have *committed no crime*. This is often referred to as a 'non-crime hate incident.'

The Metropolitan Police state the following:

A hate crime is defined as 'Any criminal offence which is perceived by the victim or any other person, to be motivated by hostility or prejudice based on a persons' race or perceived race; religion or perceived religion; sexual orientation or perceived sexual orientation; disability or perceived disability and any crime motivated by hostility or prejudice against a person who is transgender or perceived to be transgender.'

A hate incident is any incident which the victim, or anyone else, thinks is based on someone's prejudice towards them because of their race, religion, sexual orientation, disability or because they are transgender.

Not all hate incidents will amount to criminal offences, but it is equally important that these are reported and recorded by the police.

Evidence of the hate element is not a requirement. You do not need to personally perceive the incident to be hate related. It would be enough if another person, a witness or even a police officer thought that the incident was hate related.

The hate crime element is similar to that of the CPS, but the final two paragraphs are crucial here: it is, according to police, 'equally important' that incidents where no crime has occurred are *reported and recorded*. Why do the police have any involvement in an incident in which no crime occurred? The answer is an encroaching police state.

Section 4 of the Public Order Act 1986 creates an offence if a person uses 'threatening, abusive or insulting words or behaviour that causes, or is likely to cause, another person harassment, alarm or distress.'

Section 127 of the Communications Act 2003 makes it illegal to send electronic messages that are considered grossly offensive, or of an indecent, obscene, or menacing character.

Similar proposals were made in Scotland in early 2020. These proposals would sentence you to seven years in prison for the offence of 'stirring up hatred' against a particular group of people, including a religious group.

The effect on free speech of these laws is unquantifiable, they have created a society filled with people petrified to express their true feelings on a particular matter, lest it land them in legal trouble. The fact is, however, for free speech to exist, we must be able to express our views, no matter how uncomfortable that may be for others.

In this scenario, if someone expresses their opinion about a religion for example, someone else gets to decide that this opinion amounts to 'stirring up hatred,' and the opinion is quashed.

Democracy simply cannot work under these conditions. Let's return to the key meaning of democracy – the will of the people. How on earth can we know what is the will of the people if the people are not allowed to express their view? We can't. Free speech is non-negotiable if we are to call ourselves a democracy.

Here are some examples, from the UK, of the effects of free speech–crushing legislation.

First, a frightening 120,000 'non-crime hate incidents' have been recorded by police in the UK as of February 2020. The impact of being on a list of non-criminals is that these show up on criminal records – despite the fact there has been no crime. To clarify, even when a person has not committed a crime, they are still logged as having committed a 'non-crime incident' and should a potential employer, for instance, investigate a potential employee, the potential employee's name shows up on this list. It is highly likely that a person who has committed no crime will invariably be prevented from gaining future employment, and all of this simply because *someone* has said they are guilty of 'hate.'

Harry Miller is a former police officer in the north of England. Mr. Miller was contacted by police for apparently posting 'transphobic' tweets on Twitter. The police showed up at his place of work to tell him that 30 messages he had tweeted or retweeted were being logged as a 'hate incident.' There is no defence to this; it is up to the police to decide. Mr. Miller took the police to the high court and won, but again, the damage was done. People will silence themselves, keeping their true opinions to themselves, because they don't want to end up in court like Mr. Miller.

The court ruled that the police had acted unlawfully in Mr. Miller's case. However, the system would not be so kind to Maya Forstater.

Forstater lost her job at the Centre for Global Development when her contract was not renewed, thanks to the expression of her views on transgenderism on Twitter. She'd said that 'men cannot change into women,' something we would have found to be simple fact a few years ago. She took her employers to court but failed.

A preliminary hearing in central London determined whether Forstater's view that men are not women was itself protected under equality laws. It was not. The final judgement included this:

'I conclude from…the totality of the evidence, that [Forstater] is absolutist in her view of sex and it is a core component of her belief that she will refer to a person by the sex she considered appropriate even if it violates their dignity and/or creates an intimidating, hostile, degrading, humiliating or offensive environment. The approach is not worthy of respect in a democratic society.'

What an extraordinary claim for a UK judge to make. Forstater had given a view that is based upon science, biology, and until recently, would have been agreed upon by just about everyone. It is a matter of biological fact that men are not women, and women are not men, and we cannot simply become something by using its name. It is possible, using this approach, that anyone can call themselves anything and expect others to fall into line. If I call myself a tiger, and demand to live in the tiger enclosure at London Zoo, I would not be allowed to. Yet, I can call myself a man and gain entry to places and spaces intended only for men. Women doing this is rare; it is usually men who call themselves 'women' to gain access to women's spaces – something that presents a threat to women should a sexual predator take advantage (which they have and will again).

It's incredible enough that people are now demanding that we call them what we know they are not, but it's even more incredible that we can have a visit from the police, or lawfully lose our jobs, for not agreeing to do this.

The effect on free speech of these laws is unquantifiable. It is obvious the effect this is having and has had on our democracy. More alarmingly, it has become the norm across our educational establishment, meaning that large numbers of young people are growing up with disdain for free speech rather than passion for its defence. Many do not even understand its importance.

This is nowhere better demonstrated than in our universities. In the UK, a 2019 study revealed that fewer than half (ie, a minority) of students support freedom of speech. As many as two-fifths of students believe in the censoring and no-platforming of speakers. There are several examples of this exact scenario taking place, and they are not confined to the United Kingdom.

Examples of people 'no-platformed' at UK universities include me (unsurprisingly), Germaine Greer, and Julie Bindel. I have been cancelled on numerous occasions, the latest being in the University of Warwick; the Labour society there still celebrates its 'victory' in having intimidated those willing to listen with open minds to a speech. Germaine Greer is now 'un-personed' because she insists that women are women, and the same goes for Julie Bindel – both of these women are renowned feminists who argue that the 'trans' madness that has swept the Western world actually poses a threat to real women. This is considered 'hate.' What else?

In the United States, home of the First Amendment (see 'In Defence of America'), President Trump has tried to stop the rot, and force universities to embrace free speech. In March of 2019, Trump signed an executive order requiring American colleges to embrace free speech or lose funding. Any such restrictions by universities already breaches the First Amendment of the US Constitution and the left-wing anti-Trump people almost universally claimed that it wasn't needed. They would say that; it is their opponents being shut down!

Others made the claim too. Lee C. Bollinger, President of Columbia University, said free speech was 'doing just fine.' He claims this, even though he has given examples of speeches being interrupted or shut down on university campuses in the US.

Examples included that of Charles Murray, author of *Coming Apart: The State of White America 1960–2020*. The reason for the protests was largely Murray's previous book, one which suggested a genetic reason for Blacks in the US doing less well than whites (lesser intelligence was suggested). While this is not a view many people would share, it is the very kind of view that freedom of speech is *intended* to protect.

Chaos ensued at the event where Murray was booked to speak, and injuries were reported afterwards. This is how the event was later described by one of the participating students:

> *I agreed to participate in the event with Charles Murray, because several of my students asked me to do so. They are smart and good people, all of them, and this was their big event of the year. I actually welcomed the opportunity to be involved, because while my students may know I am a Democrat, all of my courses are nonpartisan, and this was a chance to demonstrate publicly my commitment to a free and fair exchange of views in my classroom.*
>
> *As the campus uproar about his visit built, I was genuinely surprised and troubled to learn that some of my faculty colleagues had rendered judgement on Dr. Murray's work and character, while openly admitting that they had not read anything he had written. With the best of intentions, they offered their leadership to enraged students, and we all now know what the results were.*
>
> *I want you to know what it feels like to look out at a sea of students yelling obscenities at other members of my beloved community. There were students and faculty who wanted to hear the exchange, but were unable to do so, either because of the screaming and chanting and chair-pounding in the room, or because their seats were occupied by those who refused to listen, and they were stranded outside the doors. I saw some of my faculty colleagues who had publicly acknowledged that they had not read anything Dr. Murray had written join the effort to shut down the lecture. All of this was deeply unsettling to me. What alarmed me most, however, was what I saw in student eyes from up on that stage. Those who wanted the event to take place made eye contact with me. Those intent on disrupting*

it steadfastly refused to do so. It was clear to me that they had effectively dehumanized me. They couldn't look me in the eye, because if they had, they would have seen another human being. There is a lot to be angry about in America today, but nothing good ever comes from demonizing our brothers and sisters.

Things deteriorated from there as we went to another location in an attempt to salvage the event via live stream for those who were still interested in engaging. I want you to know how hard it was for us to continue with fire alarms going off and enraged students banging on the windows. I thought they were going to break through, and I then wondered what would happen next. It is hard to think and listen in such an environment. I am proud that we somehow continued the conversation. Listen to the video and judge for yourself whether this was an event that should take place on a college campus.

When the event ended, and it was time to leave the building, I breathed a sigh of relief. We had made it. I was ready for dinner and conversation with faculty and students in a tranquil setting. What transpired instead felt like a Baghdad scene from Homeland rather than an evening at an institution of higher learning. We confronted an angry mob as we tried to exit the building. Most of the hatred was focused on Dr. Murray, but when I took his right arm both to shield him from attack and to make sure we stayed together so I could reach the car too, that's when the hatred turned on me. One thug grabbed me by the hair and another shoved me in a different direction. I noticed signs with expletives and my name on them. There was also an angry human on crutches, and I remember thinking to myself, 'What are you doing? That's so dangerous!'

For those of you who marched in Washington the day after the inauguration, imagine being in a crowd like that, only being surrounded by hatred rather than love.

I feared for my life.

In a mark of irony, a representative of the American Civil Liberties Union was prevented from speaking about the First Amendment at the College of William and Mary at Williamsburg, Virginia. This was essentially a protest against freedom of speech by students, apparently from the Black Lives Matter protest group. When the ACLU's Claire Guthrie Gastañaga began to speak, students chanted 'ACLU, you protect Hitler, too,' 'ACLU, free speech for who?' and 'the oppressed are not impressed.'

The ACLU defends free speech, and Black Lives Matter disapproves, because free speech involves the allowance of words and debate that they believe oppresses them. For example, Black Lives Matter later posted a video of the protest on a Facebook page, and stated, 'In contrast to the ACLU, we want to reaffirm our position of zero tolerance for white supremacy no matter what form it decides to masquerade in.' They accused the ACLU of 'hiding' behind free speech to defend white supremacy.

Finally, one of America's most prominent and famous universities, University of California at Berkeley, settled a lawsuit accusing it of discriminating against conservative speakers. According to Reuters:

> *Under the settlement filed with the federal court in San Francisco, the university will modify its procedures for handling 'major events,' which typically draw hundreds of people, and agreed not to charge 'security' fees for a variety of activities, including lectures and speeches.*
>
> *It will also pay $70,000 to cover legal costs of the Berkeley College Republicans and the Tennessee-based Young America's Foundation, which filed the lawsuit in April 2017.*
>
> *The settlement followed an April 27 decision by U.S. District Judge Maxine Chesney letting the plaintiffs challenge what they called the university's 'secret' or unfairly restrictive policies toward conservative speakers.*
>
> *She also let the plaintiffs pursue an equal protection claim over a security fee charged to host conservative commentator Ben Shapiro that was well above a fee for Supreme Court Justice Sonia Sotomayor, part of the court's liberal wing.*

This is very bad indeed, particularly in the United States, a country hitherto devoted to notions of freedom, and even with its ironclad First Amendment, America is dragged into censorship. While bad, it's no match for the UK.

The UK has no First Amendment, so we don't have any legal protection for our speech. Our laws are determined by Parliament and Parliament only. We have serious cause for worry because it is Parliament that enacted all of the free speech–restricting laws outlined above. There is no mechanism to stop this. There is no constitution that we can use to hold Parliament to account.

Theoretically speaking, of course, we can hold Parliament to account at election time, but this process is hardly flawless given the activism of the press, demonstrated with unashamed political bias of both journalists and editors.

This matters. It matters when students have little respect for free speech, it matters when the press knowingly misrepresents people's views (particularly those of political candidates of whom it disapproves), and it matters because democracy itself relies upon free speech to effectively function. No free speech, no democracy.

Still, this can be turned around. It requires a shift in political and social culture, but it can be done – we have seen societies drift in and out of democracy. We are now out, and can get back in.

The bias of the press is now widely understood. 'Fake news' is a resounding phrase of the era. CNN, BBC, and others have been found out time and again.

We can save free speech if we are all a little more like Trump, taking on the media and showing them up as often as we can. When they lie, point it out, and do it every single time. The US though, has legal protection; we, in the UK, do not. That's why I believe we need a US-like Constitution, one that will protect us from Parliament. We must repeal all hate-speech laws and tear up the police lists of 'non-crime incidents,' something lifted straight out of the Soviet Union. We must oblige universities and schools to include nationalist thinking in their debates, and we must ensure that students are able to invite whatever speaker they like, without risk of censure or violence.

If we can do this, we are saved, but Europe is not America; we have similar problems but a very different fight on our hands. We need to replace our mainstream politicians and to do so as a matter of urgency.

Populist and nation-state parties are emerging in Europe, including my own party in the UK, but time is of the essence. To save our speech, we must confront the media, the government, the police, and all parties in the mainstream political milieu.

It can be done; all it needs is democracy.

In Defence of Universal Suffrage

REAL DEMOCRACY ISN'T VERY old. When I say 'real,' I mean the will of the people, the literal meaning of the word. It was not until just under a century ago that all people were able to vote, meaning it wasn't the *voice of the people* at all, just the voice of a select few.

For example, in Britain in the early 19th century, very few people could vote. Earlier, in a survey in 1780, it was discovered that only 214,000 people were entitled to cast a vote in England and Wales, out of a population of 8 million – just 3%. In Scotland, a similar survey in 1831 showed only 4,500 out of a population of 2.6 million had the vote. This could hardly be described as the *voice of the people*.

Demands for reform littered the 18th and 19th centuries. Revolutions abroad, like the one in France, as well as literature like Thomas Paine's *The Rights of Man*, inspired the formation of campaign groups such as the London Corresponding Society who worked for the rights of all men to vote.

Fearing revolution, Prime Minister Lord Grey passed the Reform Act 1832, which gave the vote to men who occupied property with an annual value of £10 or more. This excluded six out of seven adult males and meant little improvement.

Activists continued to campaign for universal male suffrage throughout the 1800s, and although reform was made, none of it amounted to universal.

To examine in detail, therefore, the development of democracy, we must look at the development of suffrage. We will focus on two demographic groups and two countries: the rights of non-white groups in the United States and the rights of women in the United Kingdom.

THE UNITED STATES AND RACE EQUALITY

Prior to the US Civil War, the vast majority of Black people in the United States were slaves. Despite the US Constitution's claim that 'all men are created equal,' this was not quite the case in practice. Indeed, the authors of that Constitution were themselves owners of slaves. This demonstrates something key; that Black people were not considered people at the time the document was written.

When the Civil War ended in 1865 and slaves were freed, cotton, an industry that had been propped up by slaves, remained the largest export for the United States. So post-war slaves became workers – earning money for the work they had previously done for free.

The period known as the Reconstruction Period (see 'In Defence of America') would last from the end of the Civil War until 1877 and was characterized by big questions on how to take the United States into a new era. The Civil War had had the ironic effect of bringing the USA together as a nation, in a way it had not been before. Federalism grew after the war and the American identity began to be forged. However, there was still much discontent in the losing Southern states, who maintained that racial segregation and the denial of votes to Blacks were necessary for America to function. But the federal government had different ideas and began to legislate for states to enforce the principles of the Constitution – that all 'men' are born equal. This meant that the federal government imposed the requirement that Black people have the right to vote and hold office, despite protests from Southern states, including violent racial segregation groups like the Ku Klux Klan.

The era of Reconstruction had, however, gotten off to a positive start. In the years immediately following the war, three key pieces of legislation were passed. The Thirteenth Amendment abolished slavery, the Fourteenth Amendment provided equal citizenship rights and equal protection under the law, and the Fifteenth Amendment provided freedom from discrimination on the basis of skin colour. America was becoming a democracy, at least at the federal level.

The path to democracy for Black America can be summarized like this:

In the 1700s, voting was restricted to white men, and often not many of those. The original US Constitution left it to individual states to decide who could vote in elections. Across the board, however, it was white men who voted, and in most instances, only white men with property or with church membership or other religious seniority.

The 19th century brought the Civil War and constitutional amendments abolishing slavery and granting the vote to Black former slaves.

In the 20th century, the Nineteenth Amendment established the right of women to vote.

Fast forward to the 1960s, and the civil rights movement erupted. Some Southern states, still upset at the legal equality of Blacks and whites at federal levels, had introduced literacy tests or poll taxes to control voting; much of it aimed at Black communities. In the late 19th and early 20th centuries, laws had been introduced at state and local levels that enforced racial segregation. These are known as the 'Jim Crow Laws' and they defined life in the Southern states for decades. Although federal law afforded equal rights, Southern states soon elected state legislatures that would make life more and more difficult for Black people. The 'separate but equal' doctrine established by the Supreme Court in 1954 allowed the racial segregation of the Jim Crow Laws in the South because the court ruled it did not conflict with the Constitutional guarantee of 'equal protection.' That meant that Black Americans would have to take to the streets to demand change. They did just that:

Rosa Parks, a civil rights activist, was arrested in Montgomery, Alabama in 1955 for refusing to give up her seat for a white passenger. The following day, Martin Luther King Jr. called for a city-wide boycott of the public transport system. The boycott was hugely effective and lasted for 381 days. It led to the declaration of the US Supreme Court that racial segregation on public transport in Alabama was unconstitutional.

Years of activism followed, including sit-ins, marches, and rallies, many of which resulted in clashes with police. In 1963, the largest pro-human rights rally ever held in America took place in Washington, DC on a historic summer's day. It was at this rally that Martin Luther King would deliver his legendary 'I Have a Dream' speech, and this event has been credited with taking the fight for civil rights away from the streets and into law – the March on Washington was soon followed by the passing of the Civil Rights Act of 1964.

In an American landmark, the Civil Rights Act of 1964 outlawed discrimination based on race, colour, religion, or sex. Crucially, it prohibited unequal application of voter registration requirements, meaning that states could not enact local laws to make it difficult or expensive to register to vote. It also abolished racial segregation in schools, employment, and public accommodations.

Race relations in the United States are highly visible and divisive to this day. There are still regular accusations of racism, including those where none can be found. In fact, it is entirely evident that cultural Marxism has hijacked the just cause of racial equality in terms of democratic rights, and turned it into exploitation to attack Western democracy itself. For example, accusations of racism can now destroy lives in the US, just as it can in the UK. Under the fake guise of fighting racism, groups such as Antifa and Black Lives Matter use violence and intimidation to close down the free-speech rights of its opponents.

Cultural Marxism is one of the great threats to democracy, alongside the usual elitism and snobbery, and a mainstream media propping up a false narrative and interrupting the process of democracy. It refers to the Marxisation of gender, sexuality, and race, as well as class. It creates a list of victims and a hierarchy of victimhood. Those who are perceived as victims are always innocent in the eyes of the cultural Marxist – victims of oppression, endlessly and always, regardless of that individual's life experience. A cultural Marxist will assert that all Black people are oppressed, irrespective of the wealth and opportunity of Black people in the modern world. It will not let go of history, and it uses history to ensure division among races, sexes, and others.

It is a potent modern-day tool of the extreme left to cause chaos and conflict, with the ultimate aim of bringing down capitalism and with it, democracy.

There are few today who would call for Black people to be denied the vote; in fact it would likely be considered a 'hate crime.' Not so for another demographic who have had to fight hard for the right to a voice in a democracy.

THE UNITED KINGDOM
AND VOTES FOR WOMEN

While democracy literally means 'the will of the people,' for centuries, in practice, this meant 'the will of some people,' or 'the will of the rich and powerful,' but as suffrage advanced, it initially seemed to mean 'the will of men.' However, (as one might expect) as voting rights grew for men, women increasingly understood that they were people too, and the will of the people must also include theirs.

There are very few today who would argue that non-whites shouldn't vote, but this is not the case for women; in 2020, many prominent people still argue that women shouldn't vote, and the same provably false claims are used to disenfranchise women, as were used in the 20th and 19th centuries.

REASONS FOR
DISENFRANCHISEMENT OF WOMEN

Women Are Not Drafted to Go to War

'The Draft' or conscription refers to the compulsory enlistment in military service. Throughout history and throughout the world, this burden has largely fallen upon the shoulders of men exclusively. Today, only two countries (Norway and Sweden) conscript men and women under equal conditions. Despite this, however, women have served in armies, including the British army, for decades. There were 47,000 women active in the British military in 1917 (during World War I). Today, there are 13,000.

It was the post–World War I period in which the vote in the UK really expanded. Women had played a key role in the war effort and many of the men dispatched to the battlefield did so without a right to vote. The injustice of this simply became too evident to ignore, and suffrage underwent great changes as a result. It is perhaps their efforts in war that eventually brought many people round to the thought that women should vote, quite simply because – conscripted or not – war affects women too, and they should have a say.

Much has changed since the First World War. Women are increasingly serving in combat roles, and while I have no experience of military life, we are not inundated with stories about how catastrophic this has been. But whether women are serving in combat roles or not, or even if they serve in the military or not, women are still affected by war.

When the bombs of the Blitz rained down on Britain, they did not distinguish between men and women. When the death camps opened in Germany and Poland, they did not discriminate between men and women. If women are likely to die from war, then surely, they should have a say in it.

If war is the only reason to vote, should it not follow that old or infirm men should also not vote? In fact, should the vote only be available to men who do fight in wars? If that is the case, then it fails the democratic test; it is not the will of the people, but some people, under certain conditions. It is, therefore, not democracy.

It Creates Competition Between Men and Women

This argument is based on the notion that a woman is merely part of a man and not an individual in her own right. The precept is that a woman will marry a man, and he can then vote on behalf of both. Should they disagree on how a vote should be cast, then it is the man who has the final say. To do otherwise, it is argued, is to promote animosity between the husband and wife, in other words, competition between men and women, rather than cooperation.

Cooperation in this context does not mean cooperation from the male, but from the female; it is her 'duty' to submit to this will. This assumes several things. It assumes that the male is always right, irrespective of the view of the female, and it assumes that in any 'competition' between the sexes, men should always prevail. Take, for example, rights in the family. Men are provided with dominance in this context, and this dominance is deemed to 'hold the family together' by having only one person in charge; one person with the ultimate say will avoid conflict. But this argument can be used to rid us of democracy altogether. If we had an outright ruler and the people had no say, that would also avoid conflict. Democracy, in its very essence, is a competition between competing interests; proposals put forward will be voted upon, and the proposal with the most votes wins. That is competition. The purpose of democracy is to resolve that competition with ballots rather than bullets.

The argument against women voting rests upon the exclusion of such conflict from the home. Ultimately, what it means is that when men's interests clash with women's, men always win. So, in the battle against unequal divorce rights, for example, a clash between men and women erupts. If without suffrage, the woman is expected to sacrifice all of her basic rights in order to avoid conflict, rather than, say, two adults agreeing to disagree and voting as their own conscience requires – a man and a woman can come to this accommodation, just as men do between men.

Women Vote on the Left
This is a modern and hard-right view, one with (false) traction in the 21st century. The infamous American commentator, Ann Coulter, is one of the most vocal proponents of such an 'argument.' Coulter, a staunch Republican, has claimed that if women did not vote, the US would 'never have to worry about a Democratic president again.' In other words, women don't vote Republican often enough, so we must remove their vote!

Even if that were true, is this really an argument? It may be, but it certainly isn't a democratic one. For a start, is it true? No. More (white) women voted for Donald Trump in the 2016 presidential election than voted for Hilary Clinton (something many were 'expected' to do simply because Clinton is a woman, but that assumption was wrong in *that* case, as it is in many others).

In the 2015 General Election in the UK, more women voted for the Conservatives than for Labour. These facts don't seem to carry much weight with the opponents of women's suffrage. They'll instead point to studies such as the one carried out in Switzerland in 2018 which showed greater support by women for left-wing parties in Europe than from men. Crucially though, the report points out why this is. It concludes: 'Because women are more progressive than their male counterparts when it comes to social, environmental and gender issues.'

The issue of paternity leave is specifically addressed; women will vote for this it seems, and is that really so terrible? The family is crucial to society, and fathers are crucial for healthy families. Given this, shouldn't we encourage a bigger and better place for men at the family table? If so, paternity leave can hardly be seen as an evil.

Moreover, throughout history, it is the left who have fought for the rights of women, while the conservative right has, to some degree, opposed them. Indeed, in the West today, it remains those on the right (such as Ann Coulter) who oppose the very basic and essential public rights of women. Why then should women ever support them? People like Coulter will lament why her position has so little support from females, while she simultaneously denounces the rights of females. So, to use paternity leave as an example, why doesn't the right adopt the reasonable demands of women so that more women will vote for them? Instead, they demand women don't vote at all. It's entirely inconsistent and undemocratic to require that those who don't vote the 'correct' way should not vote – who gets to decide? Ann Coulter? If Coulter is to be consistent, the same argument can be used for men who vote Democrat. In other words, what she should *really* be arguing is for Democratic voters to be denied a vote.

Before I move on from Ann Coulter, I simply must add this. Coulter argues that women shouldn't vote, and when reminded that she herself is a woman, she defensively argues that women should still be able to make money (she has made quite a bit), should still be able to publish books (how she made her money), and should still be able to 'stand for office' even if women can't vote for it. Coulter is rather misguided in this belief, for how can she possibly ensure that she keeps her right to publish books and own her own money if she can't vote? It is only because she can vote that she can do everything else. She appears not to realise this and would opt to trust all of her fundamental rights to the kind of men who would take away her vote. Not the smartest move in the world, Ann.

Women Are 'Too Emotional'

Men and women are different, there is simply no denying it. Nor should we wish to deny it. The two sexes can have quite different approaches; women are generally more risk-averse than men. Men are more likely to commit their lives to work, whereas women tend to want a more varied life and consider non-work activities just as important as work. (This is why the 'gender pay gap' currently pushed by the left is a myth; women are not paid less than men for the same work but make different choices about work). Throughout history, men have been warriors: they are physically stronger than women and have a hefty instinct for protection. All these facets of men are vital for a healthy society – in other words, masculinity is essential to a healthy society, but so is femininity. That's the crucial point.

Even if we accept the above as true, does this necessarily mean that women are more emotional than men, and if so, why is that a negative and how do we travel from more emotional to too emotional? First, we must understand what emotion is. Emotion is the motivator and driver of human beings; it's what drives who we are and what we do. Emotions usually associated with men include pride, loyalty, and commitment. Women on the other hand are usually associated with sympathy, empathy, care, nurturing, and love. To suggest that men experience none of the emotions associated with women is a huge disservice to them. Of course, men love, and care, and nurture. It is just as true that women experience loyalty, pride, and commitment. In short, human beings are emotional; it is our very core. The emotions associated with both sexes are experienced by both sexes. Even if there are differences in degree, all such emotions are essential and healthy, and all are as important as each other.

When it is said then that women are 'too emotional,' what is really being said is that women's emotions are weaker and less necessary than men's. Is that true? Is love less important than pride? Of course not. They are both entirely natural, entirely human, and entirely necessary.

Furthermore, the 'women are too emotional' excuse was used for eons to keep women out of professions such as medicine, law, and politics. Now however, it has been acknowledged that so-called women's emotions make them good at, if not better at, those big professions. For example, in 2019, an eminent surgeon in the UK stated that he had worried about female doctors in his early career, but experience had made him change his mind. Dr. Henry Marsh said, 'I was a bit chauvinistic about it 20 years ago, when I started having women trainees, in the sense that I thought, "Well, they're just too nice," because it's such a horrible job in many ways. It's so distressing and you have to be a bit ruthless.' Following 30 years as an NHS consultant, Dr. Marsh changed his mind:

> Although it's a reverse sexist comment, in my experience and opinion, the average woman makes a better doctor than the average man…there's lots of bad woman doctors and lots of good men doctors. But given that such an important part of medicine is communication and teamwork, on the whole, it's a sexist generalisation but women tend to do it a bit better than men.

Two years prior, a study in the United States found that a patient was more likely to die under the care of a male doctor than a female. Women were found to be better at keeping patients alive because they 'use medical evidence more effectively.' It was also found that the sicker the patient, the better their chances of survival with a female doctor.

Suggestions as to why this might be include greater attention to detail, better communication, less competitiveness, and greater empathy. These are traits usually associated with females, the same traits previously used to keep women out of medicine. Now those very traits are causing women to excel at the profession.

The differences between women and men are necessary, complementary, and crucial to our health and well-being. Therefore, surely a healthy and balanced society will appreciate the emotions and traits of both men and women, and appreciate emotion itself. Both men and women contribute to a strong society, both bring necessary characteristics to the table, therefore both should vote. If they don't, it is not a democracy.

Women Are Not 'Used to Power'

This is a circular argument. Women are not used to having power; therefore, they shouldn't have power, therefore they can never be used to having power, therefore they will never have power.

That aside, it's not even true. Throughout history, women have exercised immense power; either through the fact that it is women who have raised the great men, or that women themselves have ruled over kingdoms and led armies. Women have also been in the workforce for centuries; none of this is new.

Women Are Less Intelligent

Are men more intelligent than women? No. Since women entered the professions, the evidence is there for all to see. Women are doctors, lawyers, leaders, and scientists, and are as successfully engaged, with equal ability, as men. Therefore, any differences don't appear to result in a woman's inability to engage in tasks that require a high level of intelligence. But what does the science say? That our brains are different, but those differences don't amount to a woman's inability to engage in tasks that require a high level of intelligence! My own conclusion: If a woman is smart enough to be a doctor, she's smart enough to vote. If she's not, then nor is any man who is not smart enough to be a doctor.

LIFE FOR WOMEN BEFORE VOTING AND SINCE

Before women could vote, their lives were rather different. Ann Coulter perhaps ought to inform herself of the history. In the UK, for example, women had no right to divorce, no rights over her children, and there was nothing to prevent her husband from using her as a punching bag.

All those rights, divorce rights, protection from violence, and the right to her own children, have all come about as a result of a woman's right to vote. Few women published books before that time either, and when they did, they often did so under a male pseudonym.

The Journey to Suffrage in the UK

The campaign for women's suffrage raged in the UK for almost a century. In addition to the Parliamentary Reform Act of 1832, which expanded voting rights. Let us now examine the road to women's suffrage in Great Britain.

1866 – John Stuart Mill, noted author of 'On Liberty,' is elected to Parliament. Mill was an ardent supporter of women's suffrage and would campaign on its behalf for the entirety of his parliamentary career. His first attempt would be to seek agreement to change the Second Reform Act of 1867, which gave rights to men depending on their wealth, to include women. He failed.

1869 – Jacob Bright MP introduces the Women's Suffrage Bill. It fails.

1881 – The Isle of Man gives women the vote.

1882 – The Married Women's Property Act is passed. This momentous piece of legislation recognised a married woman as a legal entity in her own right. For the first time, married women would have the right to own property.

1884 – Suffrage is extended to include all women who pay rent on (per annum) or own property of greater value than £10.

1893 – New Zealand becomes the first country in the world to provide equal voting rights to men and women.

1905 – Christabel Pankhurst and Annie Kenney become the first campaigners for votes for women, to be jailed (for disrupting a meeting of the Liberal Party).

1906 – The issue is debated in Parliament and women are openly ridiculed and mocked, causing anger in the women's section of the public gallery and a clash between campaigners and police. Police dragged women out of the gallery and some campaigners were appalled by the behaviour of others. Thus, the movement would split into those who believed in only peaceful means of campaigning, and those who believed in direct action and disruption. The former would be known as suffragists and the latter, the Suffragettes.

Also, in 1906, the word 'suffragette' is coined by the *Daily Mail* to deride and insult the activists. In response, the campaigners adopted the word 'suffragette' (and the rest is history).

1907 – Having been banned from entering the Palace of Westminster, a group of women tried to enter, leading to another clash with police and 75 arrests.

1908 – Half a million people answer the suffragettes' call and descend on Hyde Park for the largest protest for women's votes the country had seen. Supporters in attendance included Thomas Hardy, HG Wells, and George Bernard Shaw. Violent clashes continued between police and suffragettes throughout 1908; the favoured tactic was window smashing – including the windows of 10 Downing Street following a scuffle with police at Westminster. That same year, women in Australia won the right to vote on the same terms as men.

1909 – Imprisoned suffragettes began hunger strikes. A letter to the government signed by 116 doctors complains about the treatment of suffragettes.

1912 – Arising new political party, the Labour Party, demands universal suffrage for all citizens.

1913 – The Prisoners (Temporary Discharge for Ill Health) Act is passed. Known as the 'Cat and Mouse Act,' this legislation was in response to growing criticism from the public at the harsh treatment of the suffragettes. However, the act itself would face even greater criticism; it allowed for the release of prisoners on hunger strike, only to arrest them again when they became well.

This was also the year that the most famous of all suffragette protests took place when Emily Wilding Davison threw herself under the king's horse at the Epsom Derby. She died three days later; her death made international headlines and won widespread support for the suffragette cause.

1914 – World War I begins. The suffragettes cease campaigning to support the war effort.

1916 – British Prime Minister Herbert Asquith agrees that, given their efforts throughout the war, women should be given the vote.

1917 – The Representation of the People Act is passed. This gives the vote to all men over the age of 21, and all women over 30. The vote for women was conditional upon either a woman or her husband occupying land or premises with a rateable value above £5.

1918 – Women vote for the first time in a parliamentary election. The passage of the Parliament (Qualification of Women) Act ensured that women could stand for Parliament for the first time.

1919 – Nancy Astor becomes the first woman to take her seat in Parliament. American-born Astor won her election (to a seat previously held by her husband) by receiving more votes than her Labour and Liberal opponents combined. Also, in 1919, women enter the legal profession as barriers are lifted, allowing them to become barristers and solicitors for the first time.

1928 – Parliament passes the historic Representation of the People Act, finally granting women and men the same voting rights. Voting will be carried out by all men and women, over the age of 21, regardless of wealth or property status. The law was passed only 18 days after the death of the most famous suffragette, Emmeline Pankhurst. Unlike Pankhurst, however, her suffragist colleague Militant Fawcett would live to see women gain the vote on the same footing as men. She commented that she had been working for just that result for exactly 61 years.

The legacy of the suffragettes is not one of buttons and bows. These women had no compunction in using a variety of tactics to further their aims. They regularly smashed windows, set fire to buildings, attacked the homes of MPs, and destroyed much property – including with homemade bombs. Conversely, they were treated far harsher than petty criminals of the day, controversially receiving longer sentences than many men received for physical assaults against women. The suffragettes gained global sympathy because of the often-harsh treatment (including violence) from police, as well as appalling prison conditions and forced feeding.

When universal suffrage was finally achieved in 1928, debate raged about whether the suffragettes had actually achieved anything, or whether women would have won the right to vote after their efforts in World War I, regardless. This debate is ongoing.

So Great Britain had reached the closest relationship with democracy it had known to date. All adult citizens had the vote, all adult citizens therefore had the final say as to the direction of their country. Democracy had arrived; it was now only a matter of wondering how long it would last.

ONE LAW FOR ALL

The meaning of democracy, as repeated throughout this book, is 'the will of the people.' It's very simple then, to understand that in order for a system to be described as democratic, it must be comprised of the ability of the people to honestly express their views, and for this right to be granted to all people. But what of the end-stage when the laws are to be enforced?

If it is democratic for all people to form the laws, then by extension, it must be a democratic requirement that all are subject to the laws on an equal footing. Assuming you agree that this is the case, if a society is drifting away from equal treatment under the law, it follows that it is drifting away from democracy.

'One law for all' is not only a moral imperative, but a democratic one. In this regard, Great Britain is losing its democratic edge. The concept of one law for all has been radically diminished in Britain, and following centuries of fighting for equality, that very equality has been turned on its head. In 21st-century UK, to demand racial equality (for example), is to ignore people's 'identity' and 'lived experience' and in a bizarre twist, race equality is now denounced as racism.

In the modern Western world, there has been created a victim hierarchy. The further up the ladder you are, the more police and legal protection you will receive. If, for example, white people physically attacked a Black person, the chances of any charges, including aggravated charges for racism, are remarkably high. If a Black person attacks a white person, even if shouting anti-white obscenities at the time, it is unlikely there would be any 'hate' element introduced. This, in fact, has already been demonstrated by the courts when victims of Britain's notorious 'grooming gangs' (gangs of Muslim men who target white girls for rape and forced prostitution) were not considered to have been racially abusive, even though 'white whore' was a common insult as the girls were repeatedly raped. Police are happy to look away from the abhorrent crime of female genital mutilation, purely on the grounds of 'culture' (interchangeable with race). What is a criminal offense is not prosecuted because of the racial identity of the offender. Muslim women can wear burqas while the rest of society is expected to show its face.

One for all has collapsed in Britain, as it has across Europe – a continent with a long and tumultuous relationship with democracy. The beautiful and ancient continent of Europe is the home of modern democracy; it has a long and bloody story, and one that is unlikely to ever end. Indeed, that story continues to be written.

PART TWO:

DEMOCRACIES

In Defence of Europe

THE HISTORY OF MAN is war. If Europe is to be used as an example of the history of man, then this is undoubtedly true. Europe has been at war for centuries – with outsiders or with each other. There is a common theme to these wars: power, land, but also liberty. Europe's history is a seesaw between liberty and tyranny, back and forward, back and forward.

It's difficult to know where to start to outline the history of Europe, but it is only through understanding this, that we can understand why and how Europe can legitimately be described as the birthplace of Western civilization and the advancement of democracy.

Europe's influence on the world has been immeasurable. Throughout the globe, even today, its effects can be seen. There are, of course, huge distinctions to be made between the Europe we know today and the Europe that shaped the world. Europe today is going through what Europe has always gone through, a battle between freedom and serfdom. Whether the serfdom was to the divine rule of kings, to clergy, or to fascism, the yearning for liberty throughout European history, has made us who we are.

Before I describe the state of liberty in Europe today, let us look back to where it came from.

THE DARK (MIDDLE) AGES

Often used interchangeably with the 'Middle Ages,' the 'Dark Ages' in Europe were exactly as they sound: dark. The term was coined by an Italian scholar named Petrarch who argued that the period had produced little to no cultural or social advancement on the continent. The period is a long one – it lasted from approximately 500 to 1500 AD.

The term 'Dark Ages' is still often debated, as many now argue that it was not so dark after all. Whether dark or not, Europe at the time was ruled through a system of feudalism. In such a society, the king gave large pieces of land (fiefs) to noblemen and bishops. It was less advanced than the Roman Empire had been, but it also saw life expectancy rise because there were far fewer wars during this period. But it was the dominance of superstition over reason that often prompts the belief in the 'darkness' of the time. Europe was swamped in irrationality and superstition at the time, with debates around how many angels could fit at the top of a pin taking centre stage.

It was towards the end of the Dark Ages that one of Europe's greatest catastrophes would take place, the Black Death.

The plague arrived in Europe from Asia in 1347. Docking in Italy, 12 ships from the Black Sea were in a shocking state. Most of the sailors were dead, and those who were not were covered in black boils and leaking blood. Authorities quickly ordered the ships out of the harbour, but it was too late; the Black Death would kill almost one-third of Europe's population – around 25 million people.

As two major powers in Europe for centuries, England and France had long been at each other's throats for territory and prestige. The Black Death took place at a time when English–French wars continued to rage. A long-running period of intermittent war, known as the Hundred Years' War, continued throughout, and life for peasants and soldiers was poor, miserable, and short.

Despite its name and reputation, the Dark Ages did see some political advancement in Europe, much of it in the direction of democracy. The late Middle Ages, for example, saw the great schism in the Catholic Church, which would constitute the start of the fracturing of Christianity in Europe.

The Church had come under criticism throughout the later part of these periods, both for avoiding taxes and for failing to provide comfort

to the masses during the black plague. It signified challenge and it signified change.

Meanwhile, in England in 1831, the 'Peasants' Revolt' began
in Essex against high taxes (which were spent on war) applied by an
increasingly unpopular government. This revolt was defeated but
the seeds were visibly growing; English peasants were demanding
fairer taxes and greater rights. They were blazing the trail for
democracy.

Similarly, in Florence a few years earlier, peasants began to make
demands. So many had been wiped out by the Black Death that the
value of labour had risen, and the peasants understood this and fought
for rights.

The fall of Constantinople (1453) came when the Ottoman Empire
seized what was then the capital of the Byzantine Empire. Also known
as the Eastern Roman Empire, the Byzantine Empire long outlived its
Western counterpart. This conquest by the Islamic armies (which had
been waging wars of conquest since the death of Mohammed), finally
saw the last vestiges of the Roman Empire disappear. The Ottoman
Empire would last until the end of the First World War.

THE RENAISSANCE

'The Renaissance' is the name given to the period that followed
the Dark Ages and saw the birth of modern Europe and with it, the
modern world. This period is fundamental to the growth of democracy
in Europe because it was a time when human thinking began to divert
towards humanity and away from superstition and religious restriction. It has been described as the time of 'Humanism and Human-
ities,' which would later lead to expansion of thought in the sciences
and reason.

Humanism had begun to grow in popularity in Italy in the 14th
century. It embraced the idea that the human being should be central
to our thinking, and we should remember and celebrate human
achievement.

History.com summarises the Renaissance as follows:

The Renaissance was a fervent period of European cultural, artistic, political and economic 'rebirth' following the Middle Ages. Generally described as taking place from the 14th century to the 17th century, the Renaissance promoted the rediscovery of classical philosophy, literature, and art. Some of the greatest thinkers, authors, statesmen, scientists, and artists in human history thrived during this era, while global exploration opened up new lands and cultures to European commerce. The Renaissance is credited with bridging the gap between the Middle Ages and modern-day civilization.

Its birthplace was Florence and its legacy was world-shaping art, philosophy, and commerce. Florence itself was governed by a council whose members were chosen from a hat-full of the names of the city's elite. (Such 'representatives' were required to be debt-free, well-connected, and male!)

Elements of banking have a history that dates back before Christ, but it is the Renaissance, and particularly Renaissance Florence, that is considered the birthplace of what we now know as banking. The Medici family, a rich banking family in Florence, were one of the biggest backers of Renaissance ideas, and this period saw them supplying funds for art and cultural development. Banks did the same, even funding great Renaissance painters such as Michelangelo and da Vinci – two artists whose works signify the Renaissance today and remain the biggest names in historical European art. Da Vinci's *Mona Lisa* is today held in La Louvre in Paris and is, without doubt, the world's most famous painting. Both artists were among the big intellectual names of the period, where they were joined by Raphael, John Milton, William Byrd, Niccolò Machiavelli, Giotto, Dante, Thomas Hobbes, Nicolaus Copernicus, René Descartes, Erasmus, and Galileo Galilei.

While Shakespeare was born late in the Continental Renaissance, the new focus on humanity and human complexity influenced his work, just as the renewed classical works of Greek and Roman literature formed the basis of many of his plays. Such works were reborn during the Renaissance, having been suppressed by the Catholic Church for centuries.

While religion was still prominent in Europe during the Renaissance, science and reason were beginning to spring forward, and philosophers and artists of the time prompted the spread of independent thinking and the value of scepticism. But it was the invention of the Gutenberg printing press in Germany in 1440, that revolutionised communication and allowed Renaissance thinking to spread throughout Europe.

Suddenly, reading was not the preserve of the elite, and peasants were studying and thinking about politics and society as never before – and in doing so, threatening the power of authority and raising the status of the 'working class' majority.

Before moving on from this era-defining part of European history, it is worth noting some of its most famous names.

Desiderius Erasmus – This Dutch academic and scholar brought humanist ideas from the South of Europe to the North. He was instrumental in the introduction of humanism to politics, and famously translated the Bible's New Testament into Greek.

René Descartes – French mathematician, often referred to as the father of philosophy. Descartes famously stated: 'I think, therefore I am.'

Nicolaus Copernicus – The mathematician who first argued that the universe was heliocentric – in direct contrast to the teachings of the Church.

The Renaissance directly threatened Church power in Italy – and beyond. New thinking regarding the nature of the human condition made people think more about themselves and their own relationship with God, and the thought that the Church was not the only way to God was beginning to take root. This was propelled as European powers grew, following explorations and colonisation around the world, the height of which took place throughout the Renaissance period.

EXPLORATION

The modern-day left-wing routinely criticizes Europe's colonial history, but rarely is the continent credited for opening the world to global trade and all the advancement that came with it.

In the mid to late 15th century, Portugal was one of the world's great powers. Portugal was a major trading country, but when the Ottoman Empire cut off its routes east, Portugal began to set out to the West. It took control of various trade routes and its wealth and power exploded.

From the late 15th century, the Spanish Empire was based more upon colonialism than trade, and it controlled much of South America as well as the modern-day Western United States. This period saw the departure for new worlds of Magellan, Columbus, and others.

European exploration not only opened a new world of trade and discovered new lands, but brought new products and ideas to Europe, including debate and discussion around the treatment of indigenous peoples by European colonizers. Europe dominated the indigenous peoples it found in the 'New World' (Native American, Inca, Aborigine, etc.) largely because of its advanced weaponry and agricultural practices. It was able to explore because of its unique proficiency at sea. Timepieces and compasses, for example, were European inventions that helped its global expansion.

The Spanish and Portuguese were extraordinarily wealthy and powerful at this time, so much so that other Europeans began to copy them. France, England, and Holland began to look abroad – and sail abroad.

The 'Colonial Era' was one of supreme global power for Europe. Spain and Portugal controlled much of the Americas, the British Empire held the eastern part of today's United States, as well as Canada, large swathes of Africa, Asia (including India), and Australia, while France ruled much of north and west Africa.

Europe's global domination meant great advances in wealth at home. The continent's explorers brought home new practices, such as water boiling, which would help prevent disease, and greater food provisions (such as corn and potatoes from the Americas) leading to reduced hunger and starvation. Meanwhile, despite the advancements in humanism, the Catholic Church remained a supreme power in Europe, often helping kings stay in place by preaching that they were closer to God, and, therefore, deserved such unfettered authority.

As with much authority at the time, however, the Renaissance would witness massive challenges to Church rule and an irrevocable split in Christianity.

THE REFORMATION

Martin Luther was a German lawyer and thinker – who went on to become a monk – and he firmly believed in faith alone as the path to God. The Catholic Church at the time (and still), taught of the concept of purgatory. Purgatory, as Catholics will know, is a state that is not quite heaven and not quite hell. It is reserved for those deserving of neither fate. During the late 15th century, the Catholic Church sold (literally sold, ie, in exchange for money) releases from purgatory. In 1517, Pope Leo X offered 'indulgences' to those who helped fund the construction of St. Peter's Basilica in Rome. Luther was disgusted by this, as were many, and he wrote his *Ninety-Five Theses* as a result.

In his *Theses*, Luther challenged beliefs about purgatory and denied that the Pope had any power to release a soul from its grip. Furthermore, he argued that the Church cannot relieve people of sin, that this is possible through God alone, and sin is an internal struggle, rather than an external contrition or confession. Clearly, these ideas threatened the Church and they began to spread throughout Europe, thanks to the printing press.

During this same mid-Renaissance period, Calvinism was growing in France, also directly threatening the power of the Catholic Church. Calvinists broke from the Church in the 16th century when John Calvin denounced the Church and argued for similar beliefs to that of the Protestant Lutherans in Germany. Calvinists particularly believed in asking questions of the current order, something that the people of the Renaissance period were ready to lap up.

Across the channel in England, Henry VIII wanted to divorce his wife!

Given the revolution in the air in Europe and the challenge to political power, kings were beginning to feel anxious, Henry VIII being one of them.

He was also unhappy in his marriage to Catherine of Aragon and wanted out, but the Catholic Church did not approve of divorce, so there was only one remedy for it – Henry split from the Catholic Church and made himself head of the newly founded Church of England. His power consolidated, he was now head of the government *and* the Church.

Now that Christianity was firmly split in Europe between Catholics and Protestants, subsequent centuries would be littered with inter-Christianity wars between the two groups.

Beginning as a war of religion between Catholics and Protestants, the 'Thirty Years' War' devastated Europe, with up to 20% of the German population wiped out. In some areas, the death toll was 50%. The war was not solely religious, as were most throughout European history, it was about power; kings sending armies to conquer territories, other kings fighting to retake. The results of this war are too broad and complex for detailed discussion but, in essence, the Thirty Years' War transformed the political situation of Europe. The war ended with the Treaty of Westphalia, in which the Netherlands gained independence from Spain, Sweden gained control of the Baltic, and France was acknowledged as the preeminent Western power. It would not be the last example of political turmoil in Europe, but the Thirty Years' War is widely acknowledged as the last major religious war to be fought on the European continent.

THE SCIENTIFIC REVOLUTION

The late 15th and early 16th centuries were game-changers for Europe. As well as all of the above, the scientific revolution was simultaneously taking place. This perhaps brought the greatest threat of all to the Church's powers.

Nicolaus Copernicus was a mathematician and astronomer. His area of work was broad, but he is best known as the first scientist to put forward the argument that the earth revolved around the sun – in direct contradiction of the Church's teachings. (Ideas like these, however, date back to the period before Christ.)

Copernicus's theories were preached across Europe, and did come to the attention of the Church, but it was not until Galileo Galilei repeated the claim that the Church let its wrath be felt.

Galileo Galilei was an Italian physicist, astronomer, and engineer from Pisa. He has been called the 'father of physics' and the 'father of science' and is one of Europe's best known historical scientific figures. He studied velocity, speed, gravity, and relativity, but it was his belief in heliocentrism (the sun at the centre of the universe) and Copernicanism that brought him into conflict with the Church.

The Roman Inquisition was a tribunal system introduced by the Catholic Church in the early 1600s to punish heretics, as other inquisitions at the time had done with brutal efficiency. In 1633, Galileo was summoned to the Inquisition and ordered to recant his findings. He was found to be 'vehemently suspect of heresy,' spending the rest of his life under house arrest in his home near Florence. The Church had won the battle against Galileo, but knowledge cannot be unlearned. Despite its best efforts, clerics could not stop the advancements made during Europe's 'Rebirth' ('Renaissance' in French).

Other advancements in science during the period of the Renaissance were these:

English doctor, William Harvey, identified the heart as a 'pump' that sends blood throughout the human body and to the brain. He was the first physician to describe this in detail.

The 'Scientific Method' was developed, as well as reductive and deductive reasoning. All advanced the cause of reason, evidence, logic, experimentation, empiricism, and scepticism. Science would never be the same again.

Isaac Newton introduced his theory on gravity. Others had discussed this before, but Newton was the first to create a theory, using mathematics to describe gravity as being predictable and applicable to all things, large or small.

The challenges to Church power were not always overt during the Renaissance, but they brought about enormous cultural, social, scientific, and philosophical change in inevitably presenting a soft or stealth challenge. Throughout Europe, a system was in place known as the 'divine right of kings.' This held to the notion that monarchs were the right people to lead because their leadership was by birth, in other words, the work of God. Kings and queens were given their power directly from the heavens, and this suited Europe's monarchs very nicely indeed. Unsurprisingly, these notions began to be chipped away as Europe developed.

In England, Charles I was fond of the idea of absolute power for monarchs but, sadly for him, there was widespread support for the still-developing Parliament in London. This split between monarchism and parliamentarianism led to the English Civil War, with the Cavaliers taking on the cause of the King, and the Roundheads that of Parliament. Oliver Cromwell's Roundheads won the war and executed Charles I. What followed was enormous social change, and later the introduction of the 'Bill of Rights of 1689.' England's road to democracy was paved.

The Bill of Rights of 1689 went on to help shape the Constitution of the United States and indeed the 'UN Declaration on Human Rights' in the 20th century. It was a landmark in English constitutional law and it set out the rights of Parliament as well as limiting the power of the monarch (and how the monarch would come to reign). It provided also, for free and regular elections to Parliament as well as freedom of speech for its members. Finally, and crucially, it provided rights to individuals, including the prohibition of torture and the right to self-defence. Together with the 'Magna Carta' (drafted much earlier in 1215), the Bill of Rights is often seen as a vital part of the foundations of British democracy and it is not difficult to see why. Free speech (albeit for members of Parliament) was born, and the rights of the individual (both intrinsic to democracy) had taken root.

Around the same time was the 'Golden Age of the Netherlands.' Even then, the Dutch were viewed as perhaps the most liberal in Europe (as they are today), and were integral to the development of trade, science, and art. Holland was a refuge for free thinkers and radicals in Europe, in an early national display of Enlightenment values.

THE ENLIGHTENMENT

Denoted to be roughly the period from the 17th to the 19th centuries, 'The Enlightenment' was a time when Europe saw yet more scientific, social, and cultural revolution. Notably, it was a time of satire – artists mocked and ridiculed religious and political leaders. Ideas grew that promoted the primacy of reason and evidence. These, it was argued, were the foundations of knowledge, like the advancement of reason during the Renaissance.

Ideals such as progress, tolerance, secularism, constitutionality, and liberty spread throughout the continent. In France, the Catholic Church was undermined by demands for religious plurality and freedom of belief. Europe-wide debate on God and the nature of life took place, and opposition to slavery found a platform. Great writers and thinkers included Voltaire and Kant, and new theories on economics and individualism were enormously popular.

Adam Smith, a Scottish economist known as the 'Father of Capitalism,' forwarded his argument that by giving everyone freedom to produce and exchange goods as they pleased (free trade) and opening the markets up to domestic and foreign competition, people's natural self-interest would promote greater prosperity than with stringent government regulations. These theories gave rise to free-market economics, as well as making a profound impact on individualism – an essential element of democracy.

While Immanuel Kant, the great German philosopher, argued that reason was also the source of morality, Denis Diderot, a French writer and philosopher, provided a quote that summarised the spirit of the Enlightenment like no other:

All things must be examined, debated, investigated without exception and without regard for anyone's feelings.

Those words are still entirely relevant in the Europe of the 21st century.

Finally, a more subtle advancement of the Enlightenment was this: The Enlightenment introduced the idea of progress, the belief that life

71

inevitably gets better as time passes. This concept had never been taken for granted by human beings before.

THE FRENCH REVOLUTION

Europe in the 18th century was a place where life was better than before, and where people expected life to be better than before. War, however, still raged, specifically around land and control of trade routes. England was at war with the newly emerging revolutionaries in eastern America who, angry at taxes from the Crown, began to make demands for independence; both Britain and Spain faced rebellion in the Americas.
Meanwhile, France was watching this republic emerge in the New World and was rather impressed at the ideas being floated. The French therefore aided the revolutionaries of what would become the United States, in their war of independence against England.

The French were in a revolutionary mood. Ideas of *Liberté, égalité, and fraternité* had taken root, much of it creditable to the Enlightenment, as well as anger at the failures of both political and church leadership. France's peasants were poor, but were seemingly forever called upon for more taxes to finance yet more wars and conflicts.

In the late 1700s, France was the world's biggest power, ruled by Louis XVI and Marie Antoinette; both of whom were known for a love of their exquisite lifestyle. (Marie Antoinette famously said, 'Let them eat cake' – *'Qu'ils mangent de la brioche'* – when asked how the poor of France could be expected to survive on bread made from about 50% sawdust.)

The National Assembly, based in Paris, helped to run the country. This was not a democratically elected body; it was a committee of representatives of the nobility, the clergy, and a nominal representative of commoners, but accurately, as would later be described, the bourgeoisie.

A clash was to take place between the monarch and the Assembly in 1789 when the Assembly asked that both the Church and the aristocracy pay their fair share of tax. The plan was blocked by the Parliaments, a legislative body that oversaw taxation. The peasants revolted.

IN DEFENSE OF DEMOCRACY

On the 14th of July 1789, the French stormed the Bastille, a prison estate in Paris that had become a symbol of dictatorial rule. It would be one of the single most significant moments in all French history and is celebrated today as Bastille Day. The result? The aristocrats surrendered their feudal lords, and the feudal system collapsed.

With momentum and history on their side, the National Assembly passed the 'Declaration of the Rights of Man and the Citizen.' The document spoke firmly to the monarchy about the rights of citizens. It provided for free speech, property rights, and trial by jury. It stated: 'All men are born and remain free and equal in rights.' Furthermore, freedom of religion was guaranteed, a radical change for Catholic-dominated France.

Women also took to the streets at this time to protest for their rights. 'The Women's March' of 1789 marched to Versailles to bring the Royal Family to Paris, ostensibly in order to keep an eye on them, but while they never gained access to the king and queen, royal staff were murdered and many aristocrats began to leave the country.

Women were demanding equality, and a revolutionary book by Olympe de Gouges outlined their demands in *The Declaration of the Rights of Woman*. Women took part in political clubs and successfully campaigned to end male dominance in the family, and for equal inheritance rights.

Politically, the French Revolution changed the prevailing zeitgeist across Europe, away from the divine rights of kings, to the rights and authority of the people.

In 1790, further legislation confiscated church property and mandated the election of priests. The Royal Family, sensing what was coming, tried to flee the country but were caught. Meanwhile, Austria and Prussia sought to crush the French revolution lest their own citizens indulge in troublesome ideas.

The new French Republic began to take shape in the years following 1789. The 'National Assembly,' now the 'National Constitutional Assembly,' was developing and largely found itself split into two camps; one wanted to get rid of the monarchy altogether, the other wanted a constitutional monarchy. Those who wanted to keep the monarchy sat on the right of the house, those who opposed it sat on the left. This is where the notion of left and right of politics that we know today derived from.

It was all to come to a head in 1792, when the French, still in revolutionary mode, escalated in violent rebellion and brought down the French monarchy altogether. Louis XVI had developed the habit of vetoing the National Assembly. Tensions rose and on 10 August, 1792, armed militants stormed the Tuileries Palace. The following year, Louis XVI and Marie Antoinette were executed by way of the guillotine.

Post-revolution, France became utterly wedded to the notion of the 'general will.' Maximillian Robespierre, a member of the Constitutional Assembly, campaigned for universal male suffrage, as well as the abolition of slavery. Robespierre was a fierce revolutionary and oversaw the arrest and execution of those considered to be against the revolution. Around 40,000 'opponents' of the new France were murdered during this time.

Given his indifference to the suffering caused by his aspiration to build the perfect republic, Robespierre eventually lost support and was executed, but his contribution to the French Revolution is remembered today.

France was transformed. Nationalism and a love of French identity was nurtured, and crucially, secularism was injected into the country's DNA.

France was now a country ruled by citizens, not by kings, and these notions of democracy began to spread around Europe, as well as its global colonies. At home, Europeans began to object to the treatment of colonised peoples abroad, and particularly for an end to slavery.

One notable change to take place was the end of the exclusion of peasants from the high ranks of the military. Now anyone could reach the top, and one young soldier was to take full advantage. The name of that young soldier was Napoleon Bonaparte.

The French Revolution is one of the most significant events in world history, and certainly in the development of democracy and democratic ideals across the planet.

NAPOLEON

A young soldier named Napoleon Bonaparte used the new notions of citizenship in France to rise to the top. When he got there, he clarified and codified many of those rights. He would remove the rights of women altogether.

Napoleon became Emperor of France when he declared himself as such following a coup d'états in 1799. He had risen through the military ranks having played a pivotal role in the revolution.

Napoleon began to change the notions of citizenship immediately. He spoke not of individuality, but the sacrifice of self for the State. He changed many of the rules of citizenship and property rights.

History.com describes this as follows:

> *After four years of debate and planning, French Emperor Napoleon Bonaparte enacts a new legal framework for France, known as the 'Napoleonic Code.' The civil code gave post-revolutionary France its first coherent set of laws concerning property, colonial affairs, and family / individual rights.*
>
> *In 1800, General Napoleon Bonaparte, as the new dictator of France, began the arduous task of revising France's outdated and muddled legal system. He established a special commission led by J.J. Cambaceres, which met more than 80 times to discuss the revolutionary legal revisions, and Napoleon presided over nearly half of these sessions. In March 1804, the Napoleonic Code was finally approved.*
>
> *It codified several branches of law, including commercial and criminal law, and divided civil law into categories of property and family. The Napoleonic Code made the authority of men over their families stronger, deprived women of any individual rights, and reduced the rights of illegitimate children. All male citizens were also granted equal rights under the law and the right to religious dissent, but colonial slavery was reintroduced. The laws were applied to all territories under Napoleon's control and were influential in several other European countries, as well as in South America.*

Countries around the world began to imitate France's new legal and educational system. Napoleon introduced higher education (*lycée*) and educational standards rose across the board. He pushed back free speech but introduced censorship, and he returned many of the lost titles to the aristocracy.

Suffering from something of a 'Napoleon Complex,' Bonaparte began to set his sights on no less than conquering Europe. He did a good job. He conquered Prussia and Spain (among others) and his wars sent Europe up in flames once again. His final defeat in the battle of Waterloo saw an end to the Napoleonic era and a new start for Europe.

At a post-Napoleonic meeting in Vienna, the advancement of liberties, secularism, and reason were blamed for the tumultuous and deadly situation in Europe. It was concluded that individual rights needed to be pushed back, and obedience to the Church promoted once again.

The effect of this decision was numerous fractions and conflict within Christianity. Methodists began to emerge in England, with an anti-monarchy philosophy. Nationalism was strengthened throughout the continent and 'Romanticism' began to rise. Romanticism believed that 'feeling is superior to reason,' 'nature is superior to manufacturing,' and 'the past is superior to the present.'

Some of the gains made during the French Revolution, therefore, were soon pushed back, but the overall change was permanent. France had advanced democracy to an extent never seen before on our continent.

THE INDUSTRIAL REVOLUTION

In Europe in the 1820s, people lived largely as they had in the 1720s. Most people worked in agriculture, towns and villages were small, and horses were still the common mode of transport. In other words, there had been very little change over those 100 years. The changes that took place, however, between 1820 and 1920 were the greatest and most profound that human beings had ever known. There were more changes in that 100-year period than there had been over the previous 100,000. It all started in England and is known as the 'Industrial Revolution.'

Essentially the industrial revolution introduced mass production and factories for the first time. This transformed the British economy away from agriculture and self-sustenance, into large-scale industry.

It brought with it new machines, new sources of power, and a new working class.

With the rise of factories came a new 'class' of people, the factory workers. Professionals at the time (doctors, lawyers, etc.) began to be thought of separately from the factory worker, and what we know today as the 'middle class' came into being.

The new working class was often subjected to terrible conditions in factories; there was no health and safety and workers had few, if any rights. They worked long hours in miserable conditions for subsistence wages. The result? The rise of trade unionism and the labour movement. Workers began to form groups and organisations to argue for their own interests; these concepts spread throughout the continent (and to the United States).

The world was completely transformed.

Cars and steam engines were not far behind and the impact is obvious; suddenly there was mass manufacturing, which could be transferred across the country in bulk. Our way of living would never be the same. Cities were formed and quickly grew. This New World brought with it new politics, as workers demanded rights and the ordinary citizen was once again elevated.

Industrialisation increased political activism both in Europe and in the Americas, and Europeans began to look inward after centuries of colonialism. South America became independent of Spain in the early 1800s, and yet more revolution in France had restored constitutional monarchy and extended suffrage to 170,000 (out of a population of 30 million).

In England, parliamentary reform was taking place, and there was rebellion from Ireland (the Great Famine of 1840 had decimated the country's population, cutting it in half). Meanwhile, the British Empire abolished slavery, women were working and engaging in politics, and Marx and Engels published *The Communist Manifesto*. Demands for rights of workers expanded and extended throughout Germany.

Down a rocky road, democracy was coming, but it still had a journey ahead of it.

WORLD WAR I

In the post–Industrial Revolution world, life was unrecognizable from all that had gone before. Everything had changed, and so had warfare. World War I was about to reveal just how much.

What, exactly, paved the way to the First World War is difficult to identify, presenting some of the hardest-to-decipher series of events in history. I shall, however, do my best.

With the birth of the 1900s, Europe was a place of colonialism and internal alliances. The European powers ruled vast swatches of the world and each wanted more than the other. Europeans were, as usual, at each other's throats about territory and power. The world was one of empires, many of them facing rebellion. This is the context of the lead up to war.

Meanwhile, Serbian nationalism was at a fever pitch in the east. In the Balkans, Serbia was seeking independence from the Austria-Hungary and Ottoman Empires. It had previously tried to take control of Bosnia and Herzegovina to form a unified Serbian state. It wanted independence from the Ottoman Empire and unity with Slavic Serbs in Austria-Hungary.

In what is usually seen as the start of the war, the heir to the Austria-Hungary Empire, Franz Ferdinand, travelled to Sarajevo to inspect the imperial armed forces in June 1914. He was assassinated in his car by a Serbian nationalist, Gavrilo Princip, which led to the declaration of war by Austria-Hungary on Serbia. The internal alliances of Europe now complicated the matter because Germany entered the war as an ally of Austria-Hungary. The Ottoman Empire entered the war on the same side. Russia, however, came to Serbia's defence, making it all the messier and all the more deadly. As the war took shape, the enemies were the United States, Britain, France, Russia on one side (Allies), with Germany, Austria-Hungary, and the Ottoman Empire (Central Powers) on the other.

World War I was extremely bloody, killing millions (including the still-disputed Armenian Genocide by the Turks). It was marked by trench warfare in Europe, in which soldiers lived in the most appalling conditions, surrounded by dead bodies, disease, and subjected to relentless shots and shells. Millions would die in the trenches and for little to no gain. By the time the Armistice was signed in November 1918, 40 million had perished. Soldiers suffered extreme mental and physical damage from conditions in trenches, 'shell-shock' (a trauma-induced illness often resulting in disturbing and even bizarre involuntary body movements), and for the first time, chemical warfare.

In the aftermath, with the Allies victorious, they met in Paris to discuss the future. The Treaty of Versailles would blame the war on the Central Powers and require them, especially Germany, to make amends (other powers had made separate deals as the continent was carved into a new structure). It was this that largely led to World War II.

Meanwhile, there was a revolution going on in Russia. Bolshevism was on the rise, Trotsky and Lenin were beginning to yield power. Lenin argued for the prevention of democracy through violence and led an overthrow of the government in the so-called October Revolution. Lenin's government restricted basic rights to disenfranchise his opponents. At the same time, the Bolshevik party had within its ranks, an up-and-comer by the name of Josef Stalin. He disagreed in many respects with Lenin, but it was not a problem ultimately, because Lenin would suffer a premature death, leaving Stalin a free run. Lenin was not present at the congress in 1922 when Russia joined with other Eastern states and formed the USSR.

In social terms, Europe was rocked by the war, but social advances were still being made in the interwar period. With continuing industrialization, cities continued to grow, and young people continued to develop ideas about freedom and rights. Women, too, had taken on an enormous task in the war and hundreds of thousands were employed in munitions manufacturing. They also took on agricultural and other industrial work, as men simply weren't available. This would represent a turning point for women, who, after the war, were not content with home-making being their sole endeavour; their role in the war added great weight to the argument that they should have the right to vote.

World War I would bring much change. The death toll, the industrialised killing machine had not been seen before in history, but much worse was still to come. Europe's history would get even bloodier a mere 21 years later.

WORLD WAR II

As noted above, the Treaty of Versailles would lay blame for World War I at Germany's feet, a country already on its knees economically. The Germans were humiliated, poor, and suffering. The Treaty of Versailles compounded both the humiliation and suffering. It also placed restrictions on Germany's military capabilities and ordered it to pay reparations to the Allied Powers.

It is no surprise that Europe was politically unstable following the shock of World War I. Everything had effectively been thrown up in the air; there was something of a vacuum – into which fascism placed itself with relative ease.

In Italy, Benito Mussolini declared himself to be the only one capable of restoring order in the chaotic country in the interwar years. He became Prime Minister in 1922, quickly dismantled any institutions that hinted at democracy and declared himself Il Duce (the leader).

Meanwhile, in Spain, Francisco Franco overthrew the democratic government (with the help of fascist Italy and Germany); he also referred to himself as 'the leader.'

But it was, of course, Germany that was central to the outbreak of World War II. The humiliation of his 'fatherland' with the Treaty of Versailles was simply too much for rising German nationalist Adolf Hitler to take. An engaging and charismatic speaker, Hitler pushed his way to the top through brutality, violence, and exploiting German anger at the restrictions of the Treaty of Versailles. He also took advantage of an age-old European scapegoat – he blamed it on Jews.

Hitler's political life began when he joined the 'German Workers' Party' in Munich in 1919. He soon committed his career and life's work to expanding his role in the party, and by 1920, he oversaw its propaganda machine. This was the same year that the party renamed itself the 'National Socialist German Workers' Party,' or 'Nazi' for short.

Through the 1920s, Hitler gave rousing speeches claiming that unemployment, inflation, hunger, and economic stagnation in post-war Germany would continue until there was a complete revolution. To Hitler, all of Germany's problems would be solved if it reclaimed its dignity and threw all communists and Jews out of the country. His rhetoric would continue in this vein throughout his early career.

In 1921, he would become the Nazi party leader, turning the party into a mass movement that came to power, making him Chancellor in 1933 when President Paul von Hindenburg appointed him to office. Hitler quickly passed the 'Enabling Act,' which 'enabled' him to do exactly as he pleased; like Mussolini, Hitler came to power by democracy, and then quickly dismantled that democracy.

Having secured supreme power for himself, Hitler began to look outwards. He also started the systematic oppression of Jews.

This was life for Jews under Nazi rule:

- Not allowed to work in the public sector or professions; all Jewish lawyers, doctors, teachers were sacked
- School children were taught that Jews were *untermensch* (inferior)
- Denied German citizenship
- Unable to marry non-Jews
- Banned from becoming doctors
- Hitler's SA actively encouraged people not to enter Jewish commercial properties, and these were often vandalised (later, Jews would be prevented from owning businesses)
- Jewish children barred from schools
- Jews forced to carry identity cards stamped with 'J' (later, Jews would be forced to wear a yellow star to identify themselves as Jewish)

In 1938, 'Kristallnacht' took place. On 9 November, Jewish homes and businesses were attacked in Austria and Germany. Around 7,500 shops were destroyed, and 400 synagogues burned to the ground. Approximately 100 Jews were killed, and 30,000 were sent to camps. In 1939, the first ghettos appeared – living spaces to ensure Jews did not mix with others.

It's hard to believe that all of this took place less than 100 years ago in Western Europe. What it reveals is how fragile our democracy is, and why we must fight to defend it from fascism of any stripe, left or right, religious or secular. Tyranny is the opposite of democracy.

Hitler's expansion plans did not take long to fulfil. He soon annexed Austria and the Rhineland (in breach of the Treaty of Versailles). Leaders around Europe began to become somewhat anxious, but a policy of appeasement was adopted, and Hitler made agreements and deals with other European powers.

In a similar vein to the lead up to World War I, Europe was still a place of alliances, and the Anglo-Polish Agreement of 1939 would prove to be a pivotal one. Poland, being next door to Germany, was nervous. Hitler had by now taken Czechoslovakia, and Poland worried it might be next. So, an agreement was formed: the UK would come to Poland's defence should the Nazis threaten it.

Hitler was unperturbed and on 1 September, 1939, the Germans entered Poland. Secretly, Hitler had made a pact with the Soviet Union to share Poland, and only eight days later, Hitler claimed his prize. On the 17th of September, the USSR invaded Poland from the East and the country was divided. Meanwhile, Britain and France had declared war on Germany. World War II was underway.

It would last six years and would be among the bloodiest years the world had ever known. Weapons had advanced, and air bombings were a widely used tactic. The Germans used *blitzkrieg* (lightning war) to bomb from overhead; Britain came under relentless aerial attack in 1940 and 1941 in what became known as 'the blitz.'

Hitler made his way across Europe, occupying the Netherlands, Belgium, Norway, Denmark, and France. But it was his decision to invade the USSR that would ultimately be Hitler's undoing.

This obviously brought him into conflict with the USSR's 'red army' and the following war was especially deadly. The Nazis were initially successful and the USSR suffered many defeats and lost countless lives, but it was the Battle of Stalingrad that would turn things around to give the Soviets the other hand – partly because its soldiers were better prepared for a Soviet winter. In 1944, the Germans began to retreat, all the way back to Germany. In April 1945, the flag of the USSR flew over the Reichstag in Berlin. Germany was defeated; Hitler (and others) committed suicide.

The war in Europe was over, but that is not the whole story. During those same years, 1939–1945, Japan had also started nurturing expansionist ideas. The Japanese were on a military high, having defeated both the USSR and China in recent wars. In 1937, it invaded China.

There had long been tensions between Japan and the United States, and these increased (to say the least) when Japan sought to expand around the world. Japan's behaviour in China was brutal, and the United States enacted economic sanctions as a result. Japan was displeased and, wanting to position itself as a serious world power, it launched a surprise attack on the United States, at Pearl Harbor. The US declared war on Japan.

The war took shape as the Allies against the Axis. Allies included France, UK, USA, and USSR. Japan had built an allegiance with Italy and Germany to form the Axis.

With the war won in Europe, the war in the Pacific against Japan became the next hurdle to overcome. The war would end in a historically unprecedented military attack. Two atomic bombs (for the first time) fell on Japan; Hiroshima and, a few days later, Nagasaki. The two bombings killed an unknown number of people, but estimates reach as high as a quarter of a million.

Japan surrendered.

World War II, unsurprisingly, would have a huge impact on Europe and had significant influence in the Europe we live in today. As well as the war, the Holocaust had taken place; 6 million Jews and others would be murdered in industrial death camps throughout Germany and Eastern Europe – it remains one of the most horrifying and downright shameful acts ever undertaken by mankind.

Post-war Europe began to take shape. With the USSR and Eastern states settling with Communism, Western Europe would continue as democratic nation-states; this would include the newly formed West Germany. The entirety of Germany had been divided between allies upon the cessation of the war.

In the aftermath, big political questions began to be asked; how should we live? How can we prevent this from happening again? The result was a total transformation of European life, politically and socially, and the Europe we know today rose from the rubble.

EUROPE TODAY

> We keep on talking about the problem with democracy and the problem with the deficit, but at what point do you say, 'Actually, democracy is not as important as the future economy and stability and prosperity of the country right now.'?
>
> – Emily Maitlis, BBC

I should write to Maitlis and thank her for this wonderful quote. It so perfectly encapsulates the issue and demonstrates the mindset of tyranny; the same tyranny that ordinary Europeans have been forced to rise up against for centuries and centuries and must do so again now.

What Maitlis demonstrates is elitism. She refers to democracy as 'the problem.' People like Maitlis, the self-important 'elites,' see democracy as something they generously allow the plebs to have, at least every now and then. But when we vote in a way that doesn't suit elites like Maitlis, they demand a rethink of this whole 'democracy' business. 'They're not voting the way we want so their vote should be taken away.' That's what she should have said; it would have been more honest.

The battle between the Ruler and the Ruled is eternal. The Ruler believes that he is superior, and right, and should therefore make the decisions on behalf of the Ruled. The Ruler sees the Ruled as sub-educated, stupid, and one who should stick to menial tasks. The idea that the Ruled should be able to make momentous decisions, particularly ones that adversely affect the Ruler, is unthinkable to the Ruler. That Ruler is Emily Maitlis et al, the Ruled are those who voted against her interests in the largest democratic exercise in British history: Brexit.

'Brexit' is a word coined to represent British Exit from the European Union. On 23 June, 2016, I and millions of British citizens went to the polls to vote on our membership of the EU – should we stay, or should we go? In the run-up to the referendum, the Ruler (represented by the mainstream press who always does its bidding) did all it could to maintain its position as Ruler. The EU was the Ruler, the elite. If it could be brought down, so could the entire platform of elitism. That would never do.

The European Union is the latest attempt by European Rulers to cement their unfettered power over the lives of the Ruled. It represents the latest battle between tyranny and democracy, and the elites, as always, will fight for the tyranny that allows them to remain the elite. The last thing the elite want is to be on the same footing as the plebs; something democracy provides explicitly for. One vote is one vote – whether cast by Emily Maitlis or the person who cleans the floor, their vote is the same, and the Rulers find this intolerable. Hence 'the problem with democracy.'

The EU started at the end of World War II as a coal and steel agreement. Formally established in 1951, France, Belgium, West Germany, the Netherlands, Luxembourg, and Italy signed the Treaty of Paris and created the European Coal and Steel Community. This was an effort to pool resources of coal and steel, largely to keep an eye on Germany and disallow them building munitions independently. Germany had once again come out of war humiliated and defeated.

Soon enough, a coal and steel agreement would develop into a common market, where countries would trade tariff-free. By 2016, it had grown beyond all previous description into a European Superstate with a flag, an anthem, a parliament, and even an unelected 'president.'

The EU is elitism defined. Its only democratic body is the directly elected Parliament; an institution with no ability to introduce legislation and one which rubber stamps the decisions of the unelected EU elite (the Commission). The Parliament supplies a veneer of democracy, it is a disguise; that is its sole function.

The EU made laws that were binding on all member states; by 2016, this was 28 countries (it had stretched out to Eastern Europe in 2004). These laws were not voted upon, therefore not agreed upon, by any electorate in any European nation. They were simply imposed, and we had no way to remove or hold to account those who imposed them.

The advancement from a coal and steel agreement to a superstate governed by an unelected clique did not go unnoticed by the people of Europe. On more than one occasion, the people tried to fight back at the ballot box, and the EU elite ignored them. In Ireland, for example, in 2008, the people voted against the Lisbon Treaty, a document that would have furthered cemented elite rule and taken even more power from the people. It failed only because Ireland's constitution would need to change for the terms of the Lisbon Treaty to take effect there, and Ireland's constitution demands that it cannot be changed without a referendum. No other country in Europe voted on this.

So, the Irish people voted against it. What happened? They were forced to hold the referendum again, only this time with millions of EU euros behind it, aimed at frightening the Irish people into voting 'correctly.' The Lisbon Treaty itself had already been rejected by the people of France and the Netherlands when it was presented to them as 'Treaty establishing a Constitution for Europe.' Both countries said no, and the EU changed the name of the document (to the Lisbon Treaty) and did not ask France or the Netherlands for their opinion again. When Ireland got it 'wrong' later, they would soon be put right.

We, in Europe, knew all of this. Those of us who want freedom and democracy (and not paternalistic degradation from so-called elites), knew the Brexit referendum was our chance to fight for our democracy, to fight for a voice and a seat at the table. Make no mistake, this was not the intent. British elitism is just as elite as EU elitism. The British elite wanted desperately to stay in the EU elite, and the referendum was offered only because it was firmly believed that the elite would win. How could they not? They had all the power. Much of the press (especially the BBC who demonised Leaver voters as 'racists') was against leaving, and most of the governing elite too – including the Prime Minister at the time, David Cameron. Cameron had sought the referendum merely to put the issue to bed, to silence all those who moan and whinge about the EU; it was an exercise in shutting them up once and for all. Cameron's government openly insisted on staying in the EU, even spending our money to send a pro-EU booklet to every household in the United Kingdom. We were told in no uncertain terms: 'If you vote to leave, we are out. We will leave all of the machinery of the EU, the single market, the European Court of Justice, the customs union' – we would leave it all. We were told this because the elite did not understand the situation; they didn't understand that the terms they were using to frighten us out of leaving *were actually what we wanted.*

So, the referendum came, and for the elites, unthinkable disaster had struck; the result was to leave. It had not worked. The coordinated attempt to intimidate, bully, coerce, and insult simply had not had the impact the elite had hoped. The democratic instincts of the people guided them through the propaganda, and they knew intimidation when they saw it. They wanted their democracy back. It is precisely this that Emily Maitlis expressed such grave concerns about; democracy had produced the 'wrong' result, and the unaccountable elite leadership of Europe had been dealt a lethal blow. Democracy: 1, Elitism: 0.

Since the result, the Ruler has gone into overdrive. History was rewritten almost immediately. We went from 'If we leave, that's it, we're out' to 'Oh, but we never said we'd leave completely.' Suddenly, Brexit became 'hard' (we leave) and 'soft' (we don't), something that hadn't existed in the lead-up. Suddenly we didn't understand what we had voted for and the vote should be overturned. That battle continues to this day, and still, the UK has not left the European Union.

When the world was ground to a halt in January 2020 by the Made-in-China coronavirus (the latest biological assault on the world by China), the EU was called upon to come up with a plan to guide us through these choppy waters. It is our Ruler, after all. But no plan came. The EU was paralysed and had no idea what to do. National governments led their people through the crisis (for better or worse), leaving the EU completely impotent. This was particularly the case for Italy, a country that had taken the brunt of illegal mass migration from Africa – something encouraged by the European Union. Italians, therefore, were already becoming weary of the EU. Their beautiful and ancient country was becoming unrecognisable in parts, resembling Mogadishu more than Milan. But when the coronavirus struck, Italy was initially one of the worst to suffer (given the huge Chinese population, they were worst affected in their area of the country). The EU did nothing. In fact, the unelected elite Ruler didn't even discuss the matter until March, while the virus had been on the rampage since January.

The total ineptitude of the EU in the face of great crisis was an eye-opener for many Europeans as the Ruler was nigh-on silent throughout. National governments bore the entire brunt of the crisis, and Italians, in particular, could see this with unprecedented clarity. Italians (including elected officials) began burning or lowering EU flags and replacing them with the Italian tricolour. Italy could see what is now clearer and clearer: the EU represents the tyrannical elite that brave Europeans have fought against for millennia. It was all about power, its *own* power, and it has nothing else to offer. It exists solely for its own enrichment and benefit, and it must, consequently, keep the workers – the ones who make the money – at the bottom, powerless and weak. The elite fight against democracy, and those at the bottom must, therefore, fight for it.

Looking back on European history is a source of great pride for a European. Our ancient continent has both shaped and led the world in the advancement of democracy. European ideas of liberty and individualism have kept the powerful in check for aeons; we have fought and died for our freedoms, time and time again.

The eternal battle has been fought on European soil – and it has been won there. That soil has inspired that spirit of freedom in the children of Europe. The United States fought back against England for its independence and autonomy, showing that the instinct for democracy, among the Ruled, passed down through the generations; Europe's children were just as hungry for their liberty as Europe itself. Europe's children would fight the same fights that Europe had fought – and continues to fight.

That fight is far from over.

In Defence of America

SINCE THE FALL OF the USSR, the United States has held the status of the world's only superpower. This, alone, has made it some enemies. In Europe, anti-American sentiment has grown, and continues to grow, as 'woke' left-wingers, who accuse the US of imperialism, dominate schools and the public sector. Part of this, according to author Bronwen Maddox, is because the growth of American power usurped European powers and indeed, because American culture so dominated Europe from the 1960s onwards.

Today, it is treated more as an enemy than an ally, as an increasingly left-wing Europe turns its back on the founding principles of the US, and in doing so, turns its back on the values it helped to inspire.

THE ARRIVAL OF EUROPEANS

Its story is the stuff of legend, and indeed many Hollywood movies. It is a country that was put together based upon an idea, or several ideas, about liberty and individual empowerment. Its Constitution to this day provides the blueprint for a free, democratic, and secular nation. Inspired by English historical documents including the Magna Carta and the Bill of Rights, the US Constitution, while imperfect, reigns still as one of the most important documents ever committed to paper.

We will look at the Constitution in more detail later, but first, let's tell the story. We'll start where we did in Europe, in the 1600s.

At this juncture in history, the continent of America looked quite different. Populated by people known today as 'Native Americans,' it was a society without empire, but it was also a society without metalwork or written language. It was a tribal society that held its own class system. Despite that, land was a resource that was shared freely, and ownership did not exist. In this society of hunter-gatherers, land was appointed to people by leaders to live and work upon. Tribes often had female leaders, and early Europeans were somewhat shocked by their sexually liberal attitudes. Nevertheless, the Europeans came. Their arrival would turn an enormous continent in a completely new direction.

Legend has it that Christopher Columbus 'discovered America,' however the truth is a little less clear-cut. Some debate who exactly was first, nevertheless, much of the continent was Spanish-ruled from the late 1400s – a dominance that lasted for centuries. At its height, the Spanish Empire controlled around half of what is today South America, as well as Central America and what are now the Western states of the USA. That influence is apparent today in a Western USA dominated by cities with names such as Los Angeles and San Francisco.

Spain was looking for riches, and it found them. The European power was so wealthy that it quickly became the envy of its neighbours. Soon enough, others would want their piece of the pie. England set sail for the New World.

THE COLONIES

The English arrived in America to found the first colony at Jamestown, Virginia, in 1706. However, it wasn't the first attempt at an English colony in the New World. Sir Walter Raleigh had attempted a similar venture in 1585, but it wasn't to last. Jamestown would be the first success story and the first of many English colonies to be established over the next couple of centuries.

Instrumental in the growth of the English presence in America was the Virginia Tobacco Company. A combination of the 'London Company' and the 'Plymouth Company,' the Virginia Tobacco Company was founded by charter of King James I in 1606. It would establish colonies by offering work to those willing to make the journey across the Atlantic. Significantly, the companies were granted self-governance by the Crown – seeds perhaps of the notions of independence that would result in revolution years later.

The most famous journey of them all took place in 1620 when the Mayflower arrived at the shores of what is today Cape Cod. It had been bound for the colonies at Virginia, but strong wind sent it north, and the colony was settled where it docked. But even before departing the ship, those on board gave a glimpse of the democracy that America was becoming; they signed a compact agreeing to follow 'just and equal laws' that would be determined for them by chosen representatives.

Also, the stuff of legend is the relationship between the new English settlers (ostensibly seeking religious freedom as for one reason or another, they had fallen out with the Church of England) and the natives they encountered upon arrival. The relationship between Europeans and Native Americans was hardly a consistently cordial one, but in those early days, agreements were made and Native Americans (or 'Indians' as they were known) helped the settlers get to know the land and provided them with food. In return, the settlers threw a large feast to thank the Indians for their hospitality.

That feast is still celebrated today in one of America's biggest annual holidays: Thanksgiving.

Life inside the English colonies of early America was run on a somewhat democratic basis. For example, voting for representatives to make laws, as agreed in the Mayflower Compact, did come to fruition. *Who* could cast a vote, though, was rather limited. Only landowners could vote, but even with that criteria met, there were further qualifications. Despite many having come to America seeking religious freedom, it wasn't necessarily in ready supply.

The American Constitutional Rights Foundation describes it like this:

> *Becoming a freeholder was not difficult for a man in colonial America since land was plentiful and cheap. Thus up to 75 percent of the adult males in most colonies qualified as voters. But this voting group fell far short of a majority of the people then living in the English colonies. After eliminating*

93

everyone under the age of 21, all slaves and women, most Jews, and Catholics, plus those men too poor to be freeholders, the colonial electorate consisted of perhaps only 10 percent to 20 percent of the total population.

The act of voting in colonial times was quite different from today. In many places, election days were social occasions accompanied by much eating and drinking. When it came time to vote, those qualified would simply gather together and signify their choices by voice or by standing up. As time went on, this form of public voting was gradually abandoned in favor of secret paper ballots. For a while, however, some colonies required published lists showing how each voter cast his ballot.

Voting fraud and abuses were common in the colonies. Sometimes large landowners would grant temporary freeholds to landless men who then handed the deeds back after voting. Individuals were paid to vote a certain way or paid not to vote at all. Corrupt voting officials would allow unqualified persons to vote while denying legitimate voters the right to cast their ballots. Intimidation and threats, even violence, were used to persuade people how to vote. Ballots were faked, purposely miscounted, 'lost,' and destroyed.

Tumultuous internal relations for English settlers were not helped by the deteriorating relationship with the natives. English practices began to irritate the natives and resulted in huge changes to the culture and landscape. For example, English cattle would graze on native crops, and the English were used to privacy, something alien to the native Americans, who lived a collectivist lifestyle. While they shared land communally, the English built walls to separate themselves from their neighbours.

Tit-for-tat fighting broke out, including between natives with opposing views on how to deal with the English. Add to the mix that Europeans had now introduced firearms, 'Indians' suddenly began shooting each other. The wars that followed were frequent and brutal and drove the natives further and further away from the Eastern colonies.

Following in the footsteps of the Spanish and the English, along came the Dutch. Vibrant, commercially successful, and liberal, the Dutch made their mark with the foundation of the city of New

Amsterdam. As it was at home, Dutch rule was liberal. Both women and Blacks enjoyed rights, unlike elsewhere in the colonies. Still, those rights were largely lost when the English conquered New Amsterdam and became New York.

The New World expanded rapidly including a new colony, Pennsylvania, which was founded by the Quaker William Penn. In this colony, religious freedom was guaranteed (however this began to erode after the death of Penn), and such ideas would be adopted in the United States when it arrived. In terms of democracy within the colonies, voting systems had been established but the right to vote was largely dependent upon property ownership, or in some colonies – church membership. Voting rights aside, the region flourished; agriculture grew, manufacturing developed, and with it, big cities. People looking for prosperity in the New World continued to arrive in droves from Germany, France, Russia; the world was on its way. Life in the New World was viewed as plentiful to those in a Europe plagued with war and hunger. Food was plentiful in America, land was plentiful. For many in beleaguered Europe, America was the land of dreams.

James II came to the English throne in 1685; a year later, he combined the English colonies into a centrally governed region called the 'Dominion of New England.' Two years later, he expanded this to include New York.

THE REVOLUTIONARY WAR

England was firmly in charge of the developing new America, yet still there was a problem: with a new world comes a new identity, and those in the colonies began to think of ruling themselves. Notions like personal liberty were being discussed as natural rights, something that was God-given. The new 'Americans' began to see themselves as separate from their rulers in England. Eventually, the inevitable would happen, and they would begin to assert their independence. For example, individual colonies had already begun taxing their populations, and these taxes were *in addition* to the ones imposed from England (usually to fund its various wars in Europe). The Americans grew irritated. In response to a spirit of rebellion, the English imposed even more taxes, prompting protests across the colonies. These protests would serve as a unifier for the colonies, growing ever closer in their opposition to English taxes.

These coordinated efforts led to meetings between representatives of the colonies, who continued to speak in terms of liberties and rights; they wanted to create a new country based on those two foundations. To do so, they needed a revolution, and in 1775, that revolution began. A brutal war followed, in which soldiers suffered appalling conditions. It lasted until the British surrender at Yorktown in 1781. The Americas Library describes the British defeat:

America declared its independence in 1776, but it took another five years to win freedom from the British. That day came on October 19, 1781, when the British General Charles Cornwallis surrendered his troops in Yorktown, Virginia.

General Cornwallis brought 8,000 British troops to Yorktown. They expected help from British ships sent from New York. The British ships never arrived. That was lucky for General George Washington and the Continental army. The thirteen colonies found their opportunity to beat the world's largest empire.

During the war, slaves were promised freedom if they fought on the side of Britain, which many did. When the British left North America, it took some 100,000 freed slaves with them. Native Americans sometimes fought on the side of the British as well, but for the most part, they stayed out of it. France, however, was vehemently on the side of the developing new nation, and actively fought and funded the Revolutionary War. The French and British had fought many wars themselves, and France was only too happy to help the Americans fight a common foe.

George Washington had help from the French. The French navy kept British ships from entering through the York River or Chesapeake Bay. French troops led by General Jean-Baptiste Rochambeau also joined General Washington.

Rochambeau and Washington gathered an army of 17,000 soldiers to take Yorktown back from the British in early October. The army continued a siege on Yorktown. They surrounded the town. The siege cut off supplies. After a while, the British ran out of food and ammunition. They could not continue fighting.

When British troops departed from Yorktown, they played a song called 'The World Turned Upside Down' because that, indeed, was what was happening. Mighty Britain had been defeated by an underdog, and a whole new nation was born (well, almost). While the British surrendered in 1781, it would be another two years before the Treaty of Paris would end the war and formally recognise the colonies' independence.

THE BIRTH OF THE UNITED STATES OF AMERICA

The newly independent colonies had an enormous task ahead of them. How would they govern the united lands they had battled to gain control of? Their decisions would have an impact all over the world and would cement notions of rights and democracy never seen before.

First things first; the new colonies became 'states,' and the Church of England ceased to have any power, so religious freedom flourished. With continuing growth of manufacturing and agriculture, the economy blossomed. This new country was developing political ideals that would inspire revolution and the yearning for liberty throughout a colonised world. Those ideas were structured and clarified as the Constitution of the United States started to put down roots. The country's Declaration of Independence would state, quite clearly, the ideals upon which the new nation would develop. This included:

> We hold these truths to be self-evident, that all men are created equal, that they are endowed by their Creator with certain unalienable Rights, that among these are Life, Liberty and the pursuit of Happiness.

These notions of inalienable rights were entirely different to what was understood in Europe, a continent ruled for aeons by the absolute power of kings and clergy. Europe had given birth to America, but America cut the cord and went its own way, forged its own identity, and in turn, influenced others all over the world to do the same.

The US Constitution was not developed on a single occasion; it has been altered and added to many times. Its birth took place at a meeting in Annapolis, Maryland in 1786. Here, delegates discussed trade between the states, as well as confederation and how this would work in practice. However, as not all the new states were represented, it was agreed to meet again the following year in Philadelphia. Presided over by George Washington, the 1787 convention would ultimately lay the framework for the Constitution.

Additionally, practicalities of governance were also ironed out. The two Houses of Congress were established, as was the principle of the separation of powers: an autonomous judiciary, executive, and legislature.

Meanwhile, expansion westwards continued, and the newly formed United States expanded and prospered, all the while developing distinct and separate attitudes in the Northern and Southern states.

The development of the United States was not without its strife. Two quite different societies were developing with agriculture dominant in Southern states and manufacturing being the mainstay of the North. In terms of democracy and voting rights, federal America largely left this decision to each state, but such rights were rigidly limited. The Carnegie Corporation of New York summarises the situation like this:

> Despite their belief in the virtues of democracy, the founders of the United States accepted and endorsed severe limits on voting. The U.S. Constitution originally left it to states to determine who is qualified to vote in elections. For decades, state legislatures generally restricted voting to white males who owned property. Some states also employed religious tests to ensure that only Christian men could vote.

In the early United States, democracy existed in theory, but not yet on paper. Black people remained slaves in the new nation – and would do so until the ensuing war between North and South was fought and won.

THE CIVIL WAR

The US Civil War killed as many Americans as every other war the country has been involved in – *combined*. The bloodiest war in American history, it is also the most significant, because it created the United States as we know it today.

Following the Revolutionary War, the emerging new America was divided. Northern and southern states had long taken distinct paths, including attitudes about slavery. It is largely believed that the American Civil War was 'about slavery,' but as usual, it's not quite as simple as that.

Abraham Lincoln won the Presidential election of 1860. He opposed slavery, a catalyst for 11 Southern states to break away and form the Confederacy of the United States from 1860 – 1861.

The war was not solely about slavery; it was about the kind of country that the United States was to be. How powerful would its federal government be? Conversely, what powers would be held by the states? By the time of the war, loosely speaking, the Southern states wanted autonomy in the guise of the Confederacy and maintain slavery, while the Northern states wanted unity under a single federal government, with an end to slavery. The war began in 1861 and ended four years later, at the cost of 625,000 lives.

The Confederacy – both outnumbered and out-resourced – surrendered to the United States in April of 1865. I will summarise the outcomes:

- Constitutional amendments were enacted (see below.) These abolished slavery throughout the United States and Black men won the vote.
- The war was followed by what is known as the Reconstruction Era, which would determine how to bring the

seceding Southern states back into the Union. Many laws were passed in this era to re-integrate these states; these laws strengthened the federal government, the Constitution, and the Union.

- Federal government passed laws to protect Black people from discrimination in Southern states, some of which still fiercely opposed the abolition of slavery.

- Economics had also been a dividing line between Northern and Southern states, with the South preferring agriculture over the North's industrialization. During the Reconstruction Era, the federal government expanded industry in the South and constructed cross-country railways. The industrialization of the South would bring the country closer together.

THE US CONSTITUTION

The American Constitution is a short but detailed document setting out the exact method by which the country operates from a federal to a state level.

Additions have been made on many occasions throughout its history, particularly as democratic notions advanced. I will now cover the most vital of these in detail, particularly those that enhance or strengthen the democratic nature of the country's primary legislation.

The First Amendment
   Amendment to the Constitution, 15 December, 1791
   Congress shall make no law respecting the establishment of religion, or prohibiting the free exercise thereof; or abridging the freedom of speech, or of the press; or the right of the people peaceably to assemble, and to petition the government for a redress of grievances.

The United States is just as much an idea as it is a nation, and the First Amendment encapsulates that idea close to perfectly. It is the amendment that confirms democracy in the United States, and in practice, it confirms that any law that infringes upon free speech, freedom of assembly, or freedom of religion is unconstitutional and can, therefore, be struck from the law books.

The amendment provides the very building blocks of a democratic order:

- free speech so that the people may express their will
- freedom of assembly so that people may gather to discuss their will and persuade each other of its advantages
- freedom of religion – the freedom to believe what we wish without interference from the State. (This is an essential liberty, if we cannot believe what we believe, then our minds are under the jurisdiction of the State, if we cannot express what we believe, our mouths are under the jurisdiction of the State; neither scenario facilitates the advancement of the will of the people.)
- to petition the government for a redress of grievances, gives the people access to government, and a means by which a citizen can express their individual importance and be heard and taken seriously by his or her representatives.

This is, arguably, the most crucial paragraph of the entire Constitution, and one which guarantees – or helps to guarantee – democracy itself in America.

The Second Amendment
   A well-regulated militia, being necessary to the security of a free state, the right of the people to keep and bear arms, shall not be infringed.

This is one of the most disputed, debated, and opposed amendments in the Constitution, and Americans continue to argue about it to this day. Obviously, this is the amendment allowing Americans to keep guns, and it has been blamed for countless shooting sprees. The response of the pro-gun lobby is often the rather clever 'Guns don't kill people, people kill people' retort. They are, of course, right. A gun can cause no harm unless somebody uses it, but equally, harm by guns far exceeds injuries inflicted by most other methods (for example, a knife).

That debate will likely continue among US citizens, but what this amendment does, and *successfully*, is reinforce the independence of the citizen versus the State. Arguably, when the State is the only body permitted to use lethal force, the citizen becomes dependent upon the State for his or her security. America's Founders sought a government that could hold the whip hand over the citizen, and the ability of citizens to be privately armed assures that they do not depend on the State, and therefore are not subject to the oppression of the State itself. Whilst many may not like the idea of an armed citizenry, there is little doubt that it enormously empowers the individual. In other words, it gives the power to the people – the very essence of democracy.

The Fourth Amendment
The right of the people to be secure in their persons, houses, papers, and effects, against unreasonable searches and seizures, shall not be violated, and no warrants shall issue, but upon probable cause, supported by oath or affirmation, and particularly describing the place to be searched, and the persons or things to be seized.

This amendment is more important to democracy than it may seem at first sight. It regulates the power of the State to even the balance in favour of the citizen. The State has enormous resources at its disposal – the citizen does not – therefore, a criminal investigation and prosecution must take place with this power imbalance in mind, and the scales shifted accordingly. In ensuring that the State cannot enter our property or seize our property without just cause, is an attempt to even the balance and ensure the rights of the accused.

The Thirteenth Amendment (6 December, 1865)
Section 1. Neither slavery nor involuntary servitude, except as a punishment for crime whereof the party shall have been duly convicted, shall exist within the United States, or any place subject to their jurisdiction.

Section 2. Congress shall have power to enforce this article by appropriate legislation.

This amendment was added following the Civil War, putting into place the legal supremacy of the abolition of slavery in the United States. Its democratic credibility is obvious; a nation cannot be democratic if it allows the practice of slavery.

The Nineteenth Amendment (9 July, 1868)
   Section 1. The right of citizens of the United States to vote shall not be denied or abridged by the United States or by any State on account of sex
   Section 2. Congress shall have power to enforce this article by appropriate legislation.

The Nineteenth Amendment guaranteed the right to vote for women, putting some of the final democratic blocks in place.

AMERICA TODAY

It is very easy for people to criticize America, and they often do. The Western press particularly loves to attack its motives around the world, as well as its commitment to its values. The press has taken a particularly dim view of America since it had the temerity to elect a president of whom it did not approve. When the people of the United States decided, against all insistence from mainstream media and politicians, to elect and send Donald Trump to the White House, the gloves came off. Ever since his election, the US Press and the Democrats have been trying to have the election declared null and void. Just like Brexit, the elite did not approve of the vote, and so the vote became a problem. Democracy is under attack from elites in America, just as it is in Europe.

The New Yorker described his election as 'An American Tragedy.' How could this have happened? How is it that despite the best efforts of a lying media, the people can still have so much power as to vote for a president they don't like? It is the same response we experienced in Europe post-Brexit. People didn't know what they were voting for, etc. The snobbery inherent in modern politics was there for all to see. Disagree with the mainstream? You're an oik!

It didn't stop at name-calling. Once again, like Brexit, when America voted Trump to Washington, the elite decided to come up with a plan to oust him and to put the oiks back in their place. Democracy must be trounced, and the plan was to do it via impeachment. The strategy was to lie, and lie, and lie. The press, being as anti-democracy in the US as it is in Europe, could be relied upon to take the lead.

The US Constitution allows for the removal of a president from office if he or she is found guilty of 'treason, bribery, or other high crimes or misdemeanours' by a trial conducted in the US Senate. After this trial, Congress is to vote on guilt or innocence, with two-thirds (67%) of the vote needed to convict the president.

To impeach him, a good story was needed, and a story is what was delivered. In his book *The Fake News Factory*, David Sedgwick, he describes what 'evidence' was used to try to throw Trump out of office, and how it was fabricated by the media, including the British media (especially the BBC). The British elite not only sought to overturn British democracy, but American democracy as well.

He wrote:

When special counsel Robert Mueller delivered his long-anticipated report into alleged collusion between Donald Trump and Russia in Spring 2019, twenty thousand BBC activists ['journalists'] held their collective breaths.

Anticipating Mr Mueller was about to make its dreams come true, the BBC was apt to describe the Special Counsel in the most glowing terms e.g. 'widely respected former director of the FBI.'

His announcement that there had been no collusion between the Trump administration and Russia therefore proved a very bitter pill to swallow for fake news media outlets the world over.

After an investigation lasting nearly two years involving nearly 3,000 subpoenas and one that had cost the American tax-payer tens of millions of dollars, Mueller's painstaking investigation had turned up precisely zero.

IN DEFENSE OF DEMOCRACY

'The findings of the Department of Justice are a total and complete exoneration of the President of the United States,' said the White House.

Suffice to say the mainstream media was not impressed. Organisations like CNN, MSNBC, The New York Times, and Britain's own BBC as it turned out had been peddling the biggest political hoax ever created.

The charges against Trump were simple: he had solicited interference from Russia in his election campaign. But it had simply been fabricated by a press disgusted at democracy, and a Congress that is in bed with the press – they share an aim: an end to democracy.

But unlike in Europe, democracy will not die easily in the United States, thanks largely to its Constitution. A favoured tactic in Europe, as in the old USSR, is to label opposition politics 'hate.' Then make 'hate' a criminal offence and you cut off the lifeblood of your political opposition – they cannot speak openly for fear of arrest. This leaves the powerful to decide what is – or is not – 'hate,' allows the same powerful to decide what arguments the electorate should hear, therefore, what it is permitted to vote upon. That's the elite version of 'democracy,' and while it might wash in Europe, the US elite has that pesky Constitution to deal with. Try as they might, the American elite have not managed to have free speech designated 'hate' – at least, not yet.

The issue of 'hate speech' has come before the US Supreme Court (which interprets and applies the Constitution) on a few notable occasions. Case law has determined that all speech is protected in the United States unless it can be said to lead to 'imminent danger.' Otherwise, the courts have been brave (and largely consistent) in the defence of free speech, including specifically protecting so-called 'hate speech.' The US Supreme Court has protected the rights of Ku Klux Klan members, as far as even burning crosses in public. It also defended the rights of the Westboro Baptist Church, in a famous case in 2011.

In Snyder v Phelps, the Supreme Court ruled that 'Plaintiffs cannot recover for the tort of emotional distress based on picketing at military funerals because First Amendment protections shield this type of speech.'

105

The case was brought by the family of a young soldier killed in service in Iraq. His funeral was picketed by the notorious Westboro Baptist Church, led by Fred Phelps. Westboro pickets were known all round the world; this extraordinarily anti-gay church believes that 'God Hates Fags' and has become angry with America's tolerance of homosexuality such that every dead soldier is a sign of His wrath. They picket soldiers' funerals holding up signs saying just this.

However appalling this behaviour might be, it is exactly the type of behaviour that needs protecting, and the US Constitution and Supreme Court has done just that. 'Hate' is not illegal in America, racists and homophobes are still free to be racists and homophobes, because that is freedom, that is liberty. It may not be healthy – or even personally advisable – but it is freedom, a freedom that is essential to democracy, because only with freedom of speech can we truly know the will of the people.

American democracy may be under threat, but it remains far healthier than that of Europe at present. Attacks will however remain inevitable, and they will come from the far-left anti-democrats who dominate US universities – just as they do in Europe. To fully destroy freedom in the US, the conservative will need to dismantle the Constitution; it won't be easy, but the process is already underway.

This destruction of freedom in the US is well-demonstrated in an article in *The New Yorker* (2013). A desire is expressed to bring the Constitution 'up to date' because it originally allowed slavery and denied women the vote. This criticism remains, despite the amendments correcting both anti-democratic anomalies. In *The Week* in 2017, the Constitution was described as 'impossible to fix,' and a series of involved anti-democratic elements was debated.

There is, of course, nothing wrong with criticising or debating the US Constitution. It follows that there is nothing wrong with outright condemning it, either. That's the very free speech it is designed to protect. But it is the pattern and the motivation that must be watched. Those elites who oppose democracy will inevitably oppose the American Constitution, particularly as it does not allow them to unite with the press and determine that opposing politics equals 'hate.' This trick is crucial; it is the most important weapon in the tyrant's armoury.

The US Constitution may be old, and its authors far from perfect democrats (there is no such thing), but the wisdom behind it is still very much needed. The people must be the ultimate decider if a country is to call itself democracy. The press and elite politicians (particularly those of an authoritarian bent) have tried – and will try – to undermine the Constitution purely on the grounds of its protection of free speech; the primary obstacle to ending democracy and cementing the power of the elite. Whether it is pulling apart the Second Amendment on the grounds that 'guns kill people,' or, indeed, the introduction of modern European notions of 'hate,' those who want to bring America to an end will continue to try to do so. The eternal battle between freedom and slavery has been fought on American soil for centuries, just as it has been fought everywhere, and for all time.

In Defence of Israel

THERE ARE FEW WORDS that can rile a room of people quite like this one: Israel. It is an extraordinary reality. When the party I lead, For Britain, expressed support for the tiny Jewish state in our manifest's foreign policy section, some of those on the hard political right saw me as a traitor – how could I possibly defend Israel? Israel, they said, was 'funding' mass migration to the West and undermining our countries. I've asked for evidence that Israel is 'funding' migration to the West, but I've never received a coherent answer. Since I've never been offered any evidence, I conclude, therefore, that there isn't any. The only response I've heard is either silence, 'George Soros,' or 'Barbara Lerner Spectre.'

I've been involved in politics for around 20 years. I began my journey on the left-wing side of politics. There's a saying: 'If you're not on the left in your 20s, you have no heart; if you're still on the left in your 30s, you have no brain.' For many years, I was an activist with the left-leaning Labour party. Now, I oppose the Labour party with all I've got. In other words, I've undergone a huge political transformation in my adult life, but the one thing I've seen on both sides of the divide, the one thing that unites the far-left with the far-right is a complete contempt for Israel.

Anti-Semitism is nothing new. It is one of the world's oldest and most vicious hatreds. It also makes no sense whatsoever. Why Jews? Is it because they are considered wealthy and influential? This can hardly be said for the vast majority of Jews and is, of course, a kind of anti-Sem-itism itself. Even if it were true, is that a reason to hate? Is it envy? The

109

contempt for success that is common among those who feel beneath the successful, lashing out in response?

Over the years, I have asked for evidence for the accusations levelled against Jews. Just as my experience was in asking for proof of Israel funding the western migration in Europe, no one – ever – has offered me anything that resembles rational proof.

There is no doubt that George Soros is funding mass migration to Europe. Also, irrefutable: he is Jewish. Do these two facts mesh? There are many wealthy people funding mass migration to Europe who aren't Jewish. The leaders of the UK, France, Germany, Spain, Netherlands, Sweden, Denmark, and beyond…these countries have all welcomed mass immigration. Germany did so, quite famously; but none of them, to my knowledge, are controlled by Jews. None of these governments were elected solely by Jews either; they were elected by white Christian Europeans – the majority.

Barbara Lerner Spectre is a Jewish woman who made a video saying Europe must accept multiculturalism, and the Jews will turn Europe into a multicultural society. How many non-Jews have voiced the same position? I can point to dozens of examples in my own lifetime, and they're not all Jewish.

Hatred of Jews can be easily spotted in irrational hatred of Israel. I have come under relentless attack on both sides of the political divide. It's unfair to say that every criticism or debate around Israel is automatically a demonstration of anti-Semitism, but to assume that those who support Israel are doing so only because they are covertly funded by Israel is an act of anti-Semitism. This accusation has been levelled at me many times: Israel funds me.

To be clear, I've never been to Israel (though it is high on my list of places to visit), I've never met with Israeli officials, and I've certainly never received any funds from the country or its government. Still, it would simply be impossible to count the number of times I've been accused of being funded by Israel. It seems the reasoning is that for one to defend Israel – or see any good in it – can only be because one is funded by a devious Israel…that's anti-Semitism. There can be no denying that an obsession with Jews (and their apparent underhand-edness) can only be denounced as a hatred so irrational as to defy all common sense.

So, let us go back to the start. Let us examine the most common slurs, insults, and downright bizarre accusations reserved for the tiny Jewish state. What is Israel and where did it come from?

The nation of Israel was founded in 1948 and is the world's only Jewish state. Its size is miniscule, covering territory only around the size of Wales, and home to about 7–8 million people. Its foundations, however, go back much further than 1948.

Zionism is the movement that believes Jews should have their own state. It began with Russian Jews in the late 19th century who argued that the only way Jews could escape persecution – which was common – was a State of their own. They believed this should be located at the historical homeland of Jews in the Middle East – Jerusalem.

Under the rule of the Ottoman Empire, 'Palestine' was sought as a new Jewish homeland. Following the Russian revolution of 1905, Jews from Eastern Europe and Russia began to flee to Jerusalem. When the Ottoman empire fell following the First World War, Britain took control of the region. In 1917, the British introduced the Balfour Declaration, signifying its intent to create a Jewish State. However, due to Arab protests, Britain remained in control throughout the 1920s and 1930s. Then came World War II and the most aggressive attack on Jews ever perpetrated in modern history.

Adolf Hitler came to power in Germany, largely on the back of its economic situation. Paying reparations for World War I had humil-iated Germany; Hitler galvanized this to gain support. Germany was also severely affected by the economic crash of 1929 because of loans being called in from the United States. Investments in Germany stalled, and wages fell by 39%. Around 10,000 businesses closed every year, and Germany descended into a deep depression.

Following the defeat of Germany in World War I, many Germans were angry – they found the defeat hard to swallow – as did Adolf Hitler. Hitler refused to accept that Germany had lost on the battlefield, instead insisting the loss was due to internal traitors in the German homeland – notably Jews.

The origin of Hitler's hatred of Jews is unclear. He spent his youth in Vienna, a city governed by a virulent anti-Semite at the time. Antisemitism was common in Vienna in the early 1900s. In fact, anti-Semitism has been common throughout Europe's history; thus, it was not invented by Hitler, but exploited by him.

Jews in Europe had been persecuted since the Middle Ages, largely for religious reasons. The Christian hierarchy saw Judaism as something that needed to be crushed as a threat to Christianity. In the 19th century, religion was replaced by race and the idea that Jews were different to Christian Europeans began to take root. Even Jews who had converted to Christianity were seen as different because of bloodlines. Europe had entered genetics-based politics.

Hitler rapidly rose to power by exploiting all these factors and blamed Jews for Germany's loss in World War I – which, in turn, helped to create Germany's dire economic situation. When he rose to power and began to conquer European territory, Jews attempted to flee, often finding that nobody would take them in. Anti-Semitism had created the dangerous situation for Europe's Jews, and anti-Semitism prevented others from coming to their aid.

Later, this would spread across Europe. Jews were banned from certain professions, prevented from running their own businesses, barred from public transport and schools, and were even forced to wear a yellow star on their clothing to clearly identify them as Jewish. However, this persecution was only a stepping stone to the true horror Hitler's Nazis would inflict.

Nazi propaganda against Jews gained traction in Europe, and in 1941, the Nazis decided upon the 'final solution.' It was not enough to persecute Jews; they must be wiped out entirely. Murder became rampant and tens of thousands of Jews were shot all over Europe. In Kiev, 33,771 Jews were shot in just two days. Killing squads went on the rampage, and Jews were forced into ghettos. In 1942, the camps began to fill.

Belzec, in Poland, was the first of the Nazi death camps. These camps were formed for one sole purpose – to kill every Jew in Europe. Of the first 430,000 sent to Belzec, only two survived. More death camps would spring up, including the most notorious of them all: Auschwitz, also located in Poland. More than 1 million people were murdered in Auschwitz, many in specially constructed gas chambers.

By the end of the war, more than 6 million Jews had been murdered by the Nazis. The argument for a Jewish State was stronger than ever. It had been shown throughout history and had culminated in the most notorious atrocity in human history. It has been shown that Jews, following centuries of persecution, were simply not safe. They needed the ability to protect themselves, and this necessitated a State of their own. That State would be Israel.

It is hard to imagine that some people would object so strongly to the creation of a Jewish State, given how much the Jews had suffered. There are several Islamic States, for example, across the region, and yet these remain largely uncriticised, particularly when compared to Israel.

Following the Second World War, the United States agreed that Jews needed their own country and began to take up the Zionist cause. Britain, unable to find a practical solution, referred the matter to the United Nations, who voted in 1947 for the creation of Israel in the Middle East. On the 14th of May 1948, Britain withdrew from the territory and the nation of Israel began. It was attacked by Muslim forces the very next day. Israel managed to fight off this attack and gain more territory while doing so. In 1967, yet another war between Jews and Arabs (unhappy about the presence of a Jewish State) expanded Israeli territory – something that is still controversial to this day. Later, in the 1990s, Israel and the Palestinian Liberation Organisation, a group that had been formed to recover land lost to Israel, signed a peace accord. This envisioned Palestinian self-government in the West Bank and Gaza Strip. When this self-government began to be realised, two groups, Hamas and Fatah, fought for control. Conflict remains to this day.

(Hamas, an extremist Muslim group, has the annihilation of Jews as its primary cause.)

It is within this context then, that I'll address the following accusations routinely levelled at Israel, beginning with 'Palestine.' The accusation being that Jews stole the land that belonged to Palestinians. But is this true?

No, it isn't.

There has never been a nation called 'Palestine.' The original name of the region was 'Eretz Israel' and records show that Jews inhabited the area for thousands of years. Demographic surveys throughout history consistently show a Jewish majority in the region. Historical records also show that Jerusalem was the Jewish capital city of the Jewish people 1000 years BC. Christian records reveal that what is known today as the Temple Mount, was a Jewish temple at the time of Christ.

It was only during the Roman Empire that the area was given the name Palestina. It was named by the Emperor Hadrian who wanted to remove the Jewish identity of the area.

In the 7th century, soon after the death of Mohammed, Arab armies began to invade neighbouring lands. Islam began to dominate all the way to southern Europe, leading to the Crusades – religious wars with the aim of removing the Holy Land from Islamic rule. Under Ottoman rule, Jews were treated as second-class citizens, and to this day, the religion-inspired hatred of Jews by Muslims continues in the Middle East – and around the world.

To cut a long story short, the foundation of today's Israel was, in fact, a return of land to Jews, rather than the seizure of land by Jews.

Now that we have answered a key question surrounding Israel, let us look at some other absurd accusations aimed at Jews by anti-Semites. These accusations are currently on the upswing as the far-right and far-left in the modern West find common cause in the smearing of the world's Jews.

In April 2020, I published a video denouncing Nazism and all it stands for. I did this in response to a new political formation in the UK, Patriotic Alternative. This group believes in the preservation of the European majority in Europe. I believe in this, too. However, as if harking back to 1930s Germany, this group irrationally blames Jews for the current state of Europe. Though the senior politicians opening Europe's borders (primarily to Muslims) were not Jewish, conspiracy theories still abound – that it is the Jews who force our non-Jewish politicians to make mass-migration decisions. In other words, when no evidence of Jewish involvement can be found, it becomes a secret influence; there's no evidence because Jews hide the evidence. Jews therefore cannot win. Let's look at some of these anti-Semitic smears in detail.

JEWS RULE THE WORLD

The idea that Jews control the world is obviously preposterous, but it is held as true by more people than the civilized world would like to believe. There is the age-old image of rich Jews with their tentacles in every nation. Jews are said to control our governments through unknown means; they are puppet masters, controlling everything from behind the scenes. Before we go behind those scenes, let's look on the visible stage. Who are Western leaders – and how many of them are Jewish?

The United States is the current world leader and superpower. It has never had a Jewish president. Currently there are nine – of 100 – Jews in the US Senate. There are 27 Jews in the House of Representatives, out of a total membership of 435. While this clearly shows little Jewish influence, anti-Semites still argue that there are too many Jews in corridors of power in Washington.

In Europe, the UK is led by a non-Jew; France, Germany, Holland, Sweden, Denmark, Norway, Austria, Switzerland, Spain…all led by non-Jews. The 'Jews rule the world' notion doesn't look so healthy so far.

The typical anti-Semite will at this stage remind you that Jews don't rule from the front, but from behind. There is no evidence for this, but that's only because Jews are so devious and hide their involvement in world affairs. Therefore, we should look to world affairs to see this pernicious Jewish influence. Assuming Jews do secretly control the world, one would assume that they would do so in their own favour. If they are, they seem not to be particularly good at it. The United Nations, the home of globalism, should give some examples of this world domination, so let's look at the United Nations and its attitude to Jews.

The world's only Jewish state is condemned by the United Nations as a matter of routine. The global body unashamedly singles out Israel for criticism and blames it for the regular failings of Palestinian leadership in the Middle East.

For example, on 13 December, 2019, the UN General Assembly condemned Israel eight times in a single day, while no other country in the world was even remotely criticized in the same session.

This is not uncommon.

The following countries do not allow Israelis to travel within their territory: Algeria, Bangladesh, Brunei, Iran, Iraq, Kuwait, Lebanon, Libya, Malaysia, Oman, Pakistan, Saudi Arabia, Sudan, Syria, United Arab Emirates, and Yemen.

Notably, all these countries are Muslim, and most have utterly appalling human rights records; oppression of women and minorities are the norm, and there is little to no religious or philosophical freedom, and certainly no free speech. But the UN has as its mandate the protection of fundamental human rights across the world, while not condemning the above countries for flagrant disregard of these rights. Nor does the UN condemn these countries for disallowing Israelis. Instead, many have been appointed to UN 'human rights' committees. How odd that in a world controlled by Jews, the only Jewish State should be repeatedly condemned by the world's leading international body, a body which simultaneously invites rabid anti-Semites – who commit open discrimination against Jews – to sit on its key human rights boards.

JEWS CONTROL THE MEDIA

This is another anti-Semitic favourite. If one comes at this from the right, the modern hatred of Jews can largely be found here. There is little doubt that the Western world is swamped in mass immigration (mostly of Muslims) which is resulting in multiculturalism and the erosion of European culture. Anti-white hatred is so prevalent that the white majority in Europe are legally discriminated against, many of whom are prevented from applying for jobs. The press in Europe is absolutely saturated in white hate, and it has most certainly created a self-hatred among white Europeans, manifesting in our refusal to fight back against mass migration and the dismantling of our European identity.

White self-hatred is what makes Europe's indigenous continue to vote for mainstream political parties even though it is those parties dismantling our continent. White self-hatred is propagated via two major sources: the press and the education system.

Modern right-wing anti-Semitism in Europe has no choice but to accept this fact, but its response will be that this is the case *because* Jews control the media and the education system. Given the passion of their retort, one assumes there is evidence for this, but, of course, there isn't.

The most virulent anti-white, anti-Western major newspaper in the UK is the *Guardian*. Here are just a few *Guardian* headlines from the last few years:

> *Talk of 'anti-white sentiment' distracts from the fight against institutional racism*
> *Why liberal white women pay a lot of money to learn over dinner how they're racist*
> *University racism study criticised for including anti-white harassment*
> *Stormzy: UK is 'definitely racist' and Johnson has made it worse*
> *My fellow white people: if you're not part of the solution, you're part of the problem*
> *Revealed: the stark evidence of everyday racial bias in Britain*
> *Given Britain's history, it's no surprise that racism still infects our politics*
> *Britain doesn't care about health inequalities. For minorities, that ignorance is deadly*
> *Britain was built on the backs of slaves. A memorial is the least they deserve*
> *We have to avoid 'integration' becoming another form of racism*
> *Racism in universities is a systemic problem, not a series of incidents*
> *A new slavery museum will have no impact on racism in Britain*

That is just a taste, and the message is crystal clear: white people are a problem, they have mistreated (and continue to mistreat) non-white people, and in doing so, are completely unique. In essence, whites are guilty, perpetually and uniquely guilty, whether it be colonialism or modern-day racism. This is even though white majority countries now largely outlaw racism. Additionally, we are forever stained, and the only way to redeem ourselves? Open our borders to the world and then reduce ourselves to second-class citizens ('positive discrimination') in our own countries. That is where redemption lies, and the left-wing press tells us this daily.

If we are to believe then that the Jews are responsible for the spread of anti-white hate in the West, it should follow that there is vast Jewish influence in the *Guardian*. If there is, it is very well-hidden.

Here are some headlines from the *Guardian* in 2019:

UN calls for maximum restraint after Israeli strike in Lebanon
Israeli government accused of abandoning soldiers with PTSD
Trump and Netanyahu are playing a bigoted game of chicken
Israel, apartheid, and antisemitism
Freedom of expression on Palestine is being suppressed
Israeli police clash with Muslim worshippers
Israeli crews demolish Palestinian homes
Israeli fires threaten Christian holy site
Israeli spraying of herbicide harms Palestinian crops
Israeli minister talks about gay conversion
Syria accuses Israel of heinous aggression
Israeli teenagers held on allegations of rape

There is a common theme here, and it is relentless. Israel is bad, says the *Guardian*. This newspaper has also given platforms to Hamas in recent years. Ahmed Youse, published a pro-Hamas article on its website, with headlines including 'If we cared about peace, we would be talking to Hamas,' and 'Why now is the time to talk to Hamas.' Let's remember, Hamas has vowed to eliminate Jews based upon Islamic scripture – which demands just that.

In summary, if the Jews are controlling the anti-white *Guardian*, they are doing so very much against their own interests and the interests of Israel.

If Jews are pushing for mass migration of Muslims into Europe, they do so at enormous risk to themselves. Muslim immigration into Europe has latched on to our already poisonous anti-Semitism, and attacks on Jews have rapidly increased.

Though far from politically correct, there is evidence (not reported by mainstream journalists, of course) that Muslim immigration to Europe has led to an explosion of anti-Semitism. The mainstream likes to blame growing anti-Semitism in Europe for the rising nationalism and populism, but a survey of German Jews in 2018 'showed that a plurality of Jews who say they experienced anti-Semitic harassment said the perpetrators were Muslim extremists.'

Following terror attacks and the murder of Jews in France by Muslims, a Jewish agency reported that as many as 15,000 Jews left France for Israel in 2015, citing growing anti-Semitism in the country. This reality is all-but-ignored by the press, which is hard to explain, considering Jews apparently control it!

The BBC, Britain's publicly funded flagship media, has routinely and regularly been accused of anti-Israel bias, and with good reason. The BBC is one of the world's largest broadcasters with millions of viewers and readers on all corners of the globe. How is it then that such a major broadcaster can be so biased against Israel whilst apparently simultaneously being controlled by Jews?

Here are some accusations made against the BBC for anti-Israel bias:

The BBC is being accused of covering up Palestinian anti-Semitism after it mistranslated several times in one documentary the word for 'Jew' to 'Israeli.'

Israel's Foreign Ministry on Thursday morning accused the BBC of deliberately lying about the recent violence in Gaza and southern Israel, demanding it change a headline that said Israel killed a pregnant woman and her child in Gaza, but omitted the Palestinian rocket fire at Israeli civilians that preceded Israel's retaliatory airstrikes.

The new BBC miniseries 'McMafia' has been accused of making 'gratuitous slurs' against Israeli businessmen.

The BBC on Sunday apologized for a headline it published when reporting on a Palestinian terror attack in Jerusalem on Friday, admitting that its focus on the three slain assailants, rather than the Israeli victim, was inappropriate.

US President Donald Trump's son, Donald Jr., on Saturday called out the BBC for a headline on the Jerusalem terror attack that neglected to mention the Israeli Border Police officer stabbed to death, and focused only on the three Palestinians killed without noting that they were the assailants. 'Three Palestinians killed after deadly stabbing in Jerusalem,' read the BBC tweet.

While interviewing a Jewish woman at the Paris rally on Sunday, a BBC reporter linked rising anti-Semitism and Palestinian suffering 'at Jewish hands,' and urged the woman to see the 'different perspectives' on Jew hatred in Europe.

In short, if Jews control the media, they are failing to consider their own best interests! Of course, they don't control the media; it's an anti-Semitic trope used to blame Jews for the open-border, mass-immigration bias of the European press. The Europeans have themselves to blame, as difficult as that is for some people to accept. It is Europeans who have voted, time and again, for open-border politicians and parties. If we want our continent back, it is up to the European majority (Jews are a tiny percentage of Europe) to vote differently. More and more parties are now forming and promising to stop the mass-migration flow to Europe. Unless Europeans vote for these parties, the current situation will continue.

JEWS CONTROL BANKING

Another interesting and utterly absurd accusation thrown at Jews is that they control the world's banks, and with it, the world's money. Once again, there is no evidence for this. It's yet another anti-Semitic trope.

Let's look at the world's biggest banks. The usual target of the 'Jews control the banks' schtick is Goldman Sachs; one of the largest investment banks on Wall Street. It's true, Goldman Sachs was founded by Jews, and largely because Jews weren't allowed into other banks. As Michael Kinsley wrote in 2010:

> *There is the stereotype that Jews thrive and tend to predominate on Wall Street and in the financial professions generally. This is true, but so what? There is no mystery or conspiracy involved. Jews in Europe were excluded from many occupations for centuries. They couldn't own land and be farmers. Here, in the United States, they couldn't climb the executive ladder at big corporations. They were not welcome at investment banks run by Protestants. So they founded their own.*

A report published by the Jewish Telegraphic Agency in 1966 paints a portrait of Jews in banking in the US at that time. It states:

> *A survey of management posts in the 50 largest commercial banks in the United States, made public here today by Morris B. Abram, New York attorney who is president of the AJC, disclosed that 45 of these banks had no Jews among their senior officers; each of four of the remaining five banks had one Jew in such top posts; while the fifth had four Jewish senior officers. These figures – eight Jews out of a total of 632 bank officers – represent 1.3 percent.*

Jews are alleged to control banking today, but historically, the stats reveal a different picture.

So, what are the biggest banks in the world today? Here is a list, published by Market Insider in 2019:

10. Mitsubishi UFJ (Japan)
9. HSBC Holdings (UK)
8. Citigroup (US)
7. Wells Fargo (US)

6. Bank of America (US)

5. JP Morgan Chase (US)

4. Bank of China (China)

3. Agricultural Bank of China (China)

2. China Construction Bank (China)

1. ICBC (China)

Goldman Sachs, the bank associated with Jews and their apparent dominance of banking, does not even appear, and the four largest banks in the world are certainly not run by Jews. The real spectre of world domination stems from China, a country where Jewish influence is virtually zero.

ISRAEL IS AN APARTHEID STATE

This is yet another fantasy dreamed up about Israel. It simply isn't true. It is true that Israel is a Jewish State, and that Jews have a right to live there, but that indeed was the point. Surely, it's understandable given the hatred Jews face all over the world. Anti-Semites clearly don't like it much when Jews stand up for themselves and protect each other, but this is what Israel is all about. If Jew-haters don't like it, perhaps they ought to point the finger at themselves for its creation.

Israel is a Jewish state, but to determine if it is an apartheid State, similar to that of apartheid South Africa, we must look at how non-Jews are treated in Israel. If it truly is an apartheid State in in the mould of South Africa, then it follows that non-Jews are second-class citizens – unable to vote or participate in public life, subject to lesser rights. That is what an apartheid state would look like. It is very much not what Israel looks like.

The Declaration of the Establishment of the State of Israel states that it will:

ensure complete equality of social and political rights to all its inhabitants irrespective of religion, race, or sex; it will guarantee freedom of religion, conscience, language, education and culture.

Nothing at all like life in apartheid South Africa.

Let's continue.

The US State Department carried out a wide-ranging study of human rights in Israel in 2010. Once again, these findings do not remotely suggest that Israel is an apartheid state. Findings include:

1. The Israeli Government did not commit politically motivated killings and there are no reports of politically motivated disappearances.
2. There are numerous domestic and international human rights groups operating in Israel without Government restriction.
3. Independent media were active and expressed a variety of views without restriction.
4. No Government restrictions on academic freedom or cultural events.
5. The country is governed via a parliamentary democracy with an active multiparty system.

There are no signs here of an apartheid state, so let us look to the position of women and minorities in Israeli society.

As is outlined above, all in Israel enjoy equal rights according to the country's founding documents, and indeed non-Jews vote and non-Jews sit in the Knesset (Israel's Parliament). Indeed, 25% of Israel's population isn't Jewish at all, with Arabs making up 20% and other minorities 5%. There is also a significant immigrant population in Israel, despite far-right claims that this is not the case. According to Wikipedia, African immigrants make up around 10% of the population of Tel Aviv.

Sexual minorities also receive legal protection in Israel (its Muslim neighbours appear to prefer criminalization and execution of homosexuals to Israel's approach, yet tend to escape criticism for this from the Western left who reserve their condemnation for gay-friendly Israel).

Tel Aviv is now recognized as a global gay capital, and Israel gave equal rights to gays before many Western countries did. The Knesset banned discrimination against gays in the workplace in 1992, same-sex partner benefits were recognized in 1994, and the age of consent was equalized in 2000. Contrast this with the West Bank, in which homosexuals are persecuted and imprisoned, and it is clear who the real human rights abusers are in the Middle East.

The situation of women in Israel is by far the best in the Middle East, and is entirely unique. Women make up around 45% of the country's workforce, and women serve in the Knesset and as party leaders. They also serve in the Israeli Defence Force – including as officers and commanders. Arab women enjoy the same rights and freedoms as Jewish women. The Jewish state is the only country in the region where women can vote and stand for election and dress as they please.

Similar to the gay-rights situation, this reality is not recognized or acknowledged by the Western left.

Is Israel a democracy then? Yes, it ticks the boxes. Like every country, it isn't perfect, but it certainly isn't an apartheid state, and it certainly doesn't behave like its Muslim neighbours. The press is free, women and minorities are free, elections are free, and all citizens enjoy equal rights.

While imperfect, those are the healthy signs of a thriving democracy.

PART 3:

THREATS TO

DEMOCRACY

China

THERE ARE SEVERAL THINGS about China that are somewhat remarkable, one being its age. Chinese civilization is thousands of years old, but curiously, has changed little. For more than 2,000 years, China was ruled by emperors; often hereditary. A nation of dynastic rule, power was centralized and bureaucratic. With regularity, dynasties were overthrown only to be replaced by another. This story was repeated and consistent for millennia. Until, that is, the dynastic system finally fell in 1911 with the first Chinese revolution.

This revolution overthrew the final imperial rulers of China, the Qing Dynasty, and created the first Republic of China. The new republic formally began on 1 January, 1912 with a new constitution. China would flirt with democracy during this period, but only a select few were allowed to vote. Elections were held for regional assemblies which would then send delegates to a national assembly in Beijing. The Beijing assembly was dominated by nationalism, a philosophy that was primary in China over the following decades, and in many ways still is. China has a very strong national identity and sense of unity; the Chinese diaspora for example are expected to always act in the best interests of China, whether born in the country or not.

The country never really found its groove during this period; it never quite settled down. Assemblies would rise and fall, would prove dysfunctional, or simply fall into chaos. This continued until the abolition of assemblies in 1927 and the beginning of the nationalist one-party state. Elections at this time were abolished and would stay that way until people were considered educated enough to cast a vote. Things continued in this vein (with ebbs and flows and peaks and troughs) until 1949, when revolution again took place and the People's Republic of China was born. The new republic was announced by Chairman Mao Zedong (of the CCP) on 1 October, 1949. The Chinese Communist Party has governed since then.

China under the CCP at the time presented itself as something of a democracy-communist hybrid. Elections took place, but the candidates were all CCP and all chosen by CCP. China insists to this day that its governance is entirely legitimate, and while its people may not have a direct say in government, if that government is working in their best interests, it qualifies as something of a 'Chinese democracy.' Except it's not. Millions have died under CCP rule…it is hardly in their best interests to do so.

Today, China has risen to extraordinary heights – it now has the second-richest economy in the world behind the United States. Some believe it will soon overtake the US (as soon as 2030, by many estimates) as the world's richest, and therefore most powerful, nation. It is already hot on America's heels in terms of military might. Its rise to number one is now almost inevitable, especially given that the rest of the democratic West has cravenly turned its back on the United States and refused to remain loyal and to give it our backing. This is a shameful scenario that will see a world dominated by a country among the most lawless and brutal ever known.

China is as intriguing as it is sinister. Its name elicits a variety of reactions, from 'awe' at its manufacturing dominance, to disgust at its attitude toward life and nature. Life is very cheap in China, and the abuse of the environment and animals is almost too astonishing to believe.

China has no animal protection laws – none. It does have some environmental protection laws on the books, but with the determination to become a vast economy at the forefront of its ambitions, corners were cut. Environmental calamity has been the result. China is the world's largest polluter, by quite some distance. Polluted air has seen rises in health problems, and China's waterways are similarly toxic. The Yangtze River, the longest in Asia and based entirely within China, is the most polluted river in the world, it carries tonnes of waste to the Pacific Ocean each year, resulting in the death and destruction of countless sea creatures.

The treatment of animals in China is perhaps the most horrifying in the world. Animals appear not to be considered living beings by large numbers in China. While animal welfare campaign organisations are growing and awareness of the sentience of animals becomes more widespread, it remains a dark and dangerous place for our animal friends. The Chinese are disproportionately responsible for the endangerment of several key, and ancient, species; but no animal is spared. The majestic tiger is endangered the world over, and this is driven largely by Chinese demand for their body parts for use in 'medicines.' The 80-million-year-old pangolin is also treated as a cheap commodity and has no protection. Sharks and other sea life are also for Chinese taking, without a morsel of concern.

It is a strange reality then when one notes how little criticism China receives on the world stage. The country seems to be immune from criticism, regardless of its behaviour. That is the case even when that behaviour is revealed to the world and when it has been responsible for countless deaths because of the global 2020 pandemic – COVID-19.

Towards the end of 2019/beginning of 2020, news began to trickle out of China of the emergence of a new flu-like virus. Doctors in the country began to message each other about the virus, and the Chinese state came down hard. Doctors were visited by state agents and told to keep their mouths shut. The CCP attempted to cover up the virus, so it was not contained where and when it could (and should) have been, and instead was allowed to spread all over the world. People died from the virus, but it was the response of the world's governments that would prove the most amazing aspect of this extraordinary occurrence.

For the first and only time in most people's lives, we in the West were 'locked down.' For more than three months, Europe, North

America, Australia, and New Zealand (as well as non-Western countries) shut down their economies; all non-essential shops were closed, and people were obliged to stay inside their homes. The economic damage of this, the fallout, will be felt for generations. Unemployment has shot up, governments have spent billions supporting businesses, and further billions paying people's salaries. At the time of this writing, we still do not understand the impact, but it is stark, it is dangerous, and it is continuing.

The political impact was equally stark. As it stands (and as I write), in June 2020 in the United Kingdom, the government currently holds the right to order people into their homes, to order businesses to close, and to dictate how often and for how long we may leave our houses. We are prevented from gathering (freedom of association cancelled) and protesting (another crucial democrat right put on hold). Most entertainment has been culled; cinemas, pubs, theatres, bars, cafes, restaurants, museums, and sporting venues are all closed. COVID-19 saw the biggest power grab by Western governments that any of us have ever seen. China is responsible. Furthermore, it has not been held to account, quite the opposite.

When President Trump referred to COVID-19 as the 'Chinese virus' he was roundly criticized. The UN insisted that no country was to blame and even helped the Chinese government to lie about the nature of the disease, when it tweeted that the disease was not contagious between humans. This delayed a response to the virus by further weeks, exacerbating its devastating impact.

What may come as a surprise to some, this was the not the first time a disease borne in China would infect the world. The SARS disease in the early 2000s killed more than 800; this too originated in China. The bigger surprise is the major past pandemics also now believed to have been 'made in China.' The Spanish flu of 1918, which killed an estimated 50 million people, also originated there, and even more surprisingly, it is now believed that the Black Death (*yes*, the Black Death) also emerged from China. Its death toll is not known, but tens of millions died over several years.

China has taken no responsibility for the death and destruction caused by these viruses. It is a nation simply above the law and above the rules. This can nowhere better be seen than in its current day business practices. China is a law unto itself, and it is never held to account.

The business practices of China would also shock most Westerners. In his book *Poorly Made in China*, Paul Midler describes his experiences dealing with Chinese manufacturers. Manufacturing is the backbone of China's near-miraculous economic rise; it manufactures almost everything!

Midler describes how Chinese manufacturers appear to have little to no understanding of contractual obligation. Orders and specifications would be agreed upon, but the manufacturer often simply changed these without consultation. Faulty orders would be shipped and little to no responsibility taken afterwards. Stories of bad hygiene practices were common and there were few if any workers' rights and protections. But it is perhaps China's disregard for copyright or intellectual property that is most shocking. Chinese businesses openly steal intellectual property, and forgeries and copies (or 'knock-offs') are the norm.

In *Stealth War: How China Took Over While America's Elite Slept*, Robert Spalding describes this in detail. He also describes China's plans for world domination, and the enormous influence it has already established in the Western world. China is imposing its will throughout the world, and it is allowed to do so. It intends to destroy democracy everywhere and is well on the way to doing so unless it is actively stopped in its tracks.

Spalding describes in detail how China has pretended to be on board with free-market economics, and duped America into thinking it is playing a fair game. The financial possibilities in China appear endless, and are offered cheap. This has been an intoxicating draw for the US and the Western world in general. China buys and buys, the world over, and then exerts the power that comes with those purchases. Trade deals have drawn in politicians and big businesses desperate to reach the Chinese market, but it has come at a frightening cost.

China now provides more than 90% of America's medical supplies. The result is that America has gotten itself into such a predicament that it cannot (or will not) confront China about its business practices, despite the harm these do to US companies. Product forgery is big business in China, and many new firms with patented products still find cheap reproductions for sale, particularly online, which affect profits to the extent of wiping the company out. There is nothing they can do. China does not answer for this (or much else). Spalding details the influence that China is gaining among the rich and connected in the United States. China makes huge business deals, very attractive business deals, which draws people in permanently. China is buying influence, and its plan is working. Few in politics will criticize this country; so much money is at stake. Meanwhile, manufacturing has left the West and decimated working-class communities. Our homes are awash with cheap Chinese produce and this has created a wasteful throwaway culture.

Spalding highlights a couple of specific cases that demonstrate the price America is paying for cheap Chinese products; one cost has been – and will continue to be – freedom of speech.

An independent radio channel, intended to inform Americans about world affairs, was due to carry out an interview with real estate businessman Guo Wengui in 2017. Wengui is a critic of the CCP and the interview was to be conducted by Sasha Gong, chief of the Mandarin service within the Voice of America organisation.

Gong was excited by such an interview, but her excitement was short-lived. The CCP learned of the interview, and following much insistence (and gaslighting), the interview was cancelled. The CCP was calling the shots and controlling the content of an American radio station. That's not all, Gong was fired for her attempts.

In a second example, a worker in an American hotel 'liked' a tweet on Twitter that was critical of the CCP. He was fired.

This is serious. China has managed to usurp America's crucial First Amendment to free speech, which is brushed aside by Americans themselves in order to placate the tyranny of China. As its influence grows, so will this behaviour, and the prospect of a China-led world becomes ever more alarming.

In summary, China is a brutal totalitarian dictatorship that ignores contract, law, hygiene, workers' rights, environmental laws, animal rights laws, and copyright laws, to name just a few. It has been responsible for spreading diseases that have killed millions and crippled economies, without any redress. It destroys businesses with spying and corporate sabotage and is simply allowed to do so. Chinese companies will happily breach contracts and deliver substandard products, again, without being asked to take any responsibility. It is hot on the heels of America, and yet, America is going out of its way to help it succeed. Even products posted from China are delivered cheaply in America because the US Postal Service ships for them at a fraction of the cost borne by an American company. Why? Because the cost of their shipping is subsidized.

Forbes describes this as follows:

> *These super low shipping rates are being subsidized by the U.S. Postal Service. Yes, the United States and, in a roundabout way, the U.S. taxpayer is footing the bill so that Chinese merchants can ship their products to the USA for dirt cheap, essentially losing millions to support a dynamic where domestic American businesses are being undercut by foreign merchants who are immune to any and all intellectual property and consumer safety laws.*

In China, there is brutal suppression of free speech and citizens do not have the right to vote or in any way hold their leaders to account. It is a country where arbitrary execution and 'disappearances' are frequent, and it is even known that China has harvested the organs of Falun Gong practitioners for sale across the world. Indeed, organs can be ordered specifically, and the prisoner killed just in time for transplant to take place. Falun Gong is a spiritual movement, severely repressed in China. It is also known that concentration camps hold prisoners of conscience to this day (e.g., Uighur Muslims).

Horrors are frequently reported from this secretive and insular state, and yet, nothing is done on the world stage to prevent its behaviour.

Ultimately it is the cowardice and greed for cheap Chinese products that could well produce the demise of the West, bring an end to the age of America, and usher in the dark era of China.

Islam

THE ORGANISATION OF ISLAMIC Cooperation (OIC) has 57 members. These consist of 56 either Muslim-majority nations (or ones with very large Muslim populations), with the addition of 'Palestine.'

The United Nations' goal is to bring human rights to the world, and to facilitate peace and avoid war. The UN Declaration on Human Rights was not adopted by many Muslim countries because the human rights on display conflict with Sharia law – the legal system inherent within Islam.

Instead, the Cairo Declaration of Human Rights was produced, in 1990, by the OIC. This was a list of 'human rights' that were nothing of the kind because the simple fact is that Sharia law and human rights (as they are understood by all except Islam) are incompatible. Even though Islamic law was incompatible with the human rights the United Nations was formed to defend, Islamic countries not only are still members of the United Nations, but even sit on its human rights boards. One must wonder, then, why the UN bothered to formulate a list of human rights if it wasn't going to require members to follow them. In most cases it does – the UN is very quick to criticize the United States or Israel, even when they have not committed human rights abuses – but not with Islam. Islam gets a free ride. The reason is simple: Islam's global power.

It's simple: Islam is a bully. It demands that the world bend to its will, and currently, the world is doing just that.

The two main incompatibilities of Islam with democracy are its attitude to equality and its murderous opposition to freedom of speech.

Despite this, it is accommodated in all Western societies to the point where those societies are breaching their own laws and values. Islam is eroding our democracy by stealth.

Back at the United Nations, Secretary-General António Guterres told the OIC that 'Islamophobia' was his 'top priority.' 'Islamophobia' is a dishonest notion which holds that those critical of Islam are guilty of 'bigotry,' 'hate,' or even 'racism.' This is obviously absurd. Islam is a religion and criticism of religion is a thoroughly crucial element of freedom of speech. Indeed, our great democracies, particularly in Europe, shed blood for centuries for just this right. Now, with the arrival of 'Islamophobia' in Europe, we have turned our backs on our democracy in its name.

This erosion of democracy in the name of Islam, however, as can be seen from the comments of the UN secretary general, has managed to bring Western governments into line, and the media is 100% complicit.

On its website, the OIC boasts about its inclusion in global efforts for peace and equality, and the UN laps it up. In one article on its home page is featured the following:

The Security Council today recognized and encouraged the active contribution of the Organization of Islamic Cooperation (OIC) in the work of the United Nations in the fields of peace-making, preventive diplomacy, peace-keeping and peacebuilding.

'The Council notes the commitment of both the United Nations and the Organization of Islamic Cooperation to foster a global dialogue for the promotion of tolerance and peace, and calls for enhanced cooperation to promote better understanding across countries, cultures and civilizations,' according to the statement.

The 15-member UN Security Council 'has primary responsibility for the maintenance of international peace and security.' It hopes to achieve this, somehow, with the partnership and cooperation of the Islamic world. So, who exactly does the UN want to create peace with?

Algeria, Benin, Burkina Faso, Cameroon, Chad, Comoros, Djibouti, Egypt, Gabon, Gambia, Guinea, Guinea-Bissau, Ivory Coast, Libya, Mali, Mauritania, Morocco, Mozambique, Niger, Nigeria, Senegal, Sierra Leone, Somalia, Sudan, Togo, Tunisia, Uganda, Afghanistan, Azerbaijan, Bahrain, Bangladesh, Brunei, Indonesia, Iran, Iraq, Jordan, Kazakhstan, Kuwait, Kyrgyzstan, Lebanon, Malaysia, Maldives, Oman, Pakistan, Palestine, Qatar, Saudi Arabia, Syria, Tajikistan, Turkey, Turkmenistan, United Arab Emirates, Uzbekistan, Yemen, Albania, Guyana, and Suriname.

These are the countries of the OIC, and the countries that the UN intends to build world peace with! While most of these countries are small and poor and pose little threat to anyone, not so with all of them. Let's take a look at just a couple.

Iran

IRAN IS ONE OF the world's primary sponsors of terrorism. It has stated its intent to wipe democratic Israel from the map, and its proxy terror groups exhibit immense power across the Middle East. Iran is accused – and widely believed – of providing the power behind Hamas, Hezbollah, and other Islamist terror groups.

In 2011, following the terror attack on US embassies in Africa (Kenya and Tanzania), a US federal court found Iran responsible. Judge John D. Bates wrote 'Prior to their meetings with Iranian officials and agents, Bin Laden and al Qaeda did not possess the technical expertise required to carry out the embassy bombings in Nairobi and Dar es Salaam.'

Iran has been developing nuclear technology since the 1970s, something that has led to widespread among world leaders, particularly Israel. Iran has insisted its nuclear ambitions are peaceful, but its actions around the world prove otherwise.

Pakistan

PAKISTAN IS A BRUTAL Islamic state where equality is forbidden and free speech is blasphemous. In Pakistan, a person can be killed either by a mob or by a court for any perceived sleight against Islam. Famously, a Christian woman, Asia Bibi, was accused of blasphemy and sentenced to death. She had no defence because, as a Christian, her testimony is worth less than a Muslim's, and it was Muslims making the accusations against her.

Convicted in 2010, Bibi was eventually acquitted eight years later, but not because of any problem with her execution *in theory*; it was merely a finding of 'insufficient evidence.' The notion that a person should not be executed for blasphemy isn't (and wasn't) entertained in Pakistan. Indeed, to get a Pakistani passport, one would have to formally denounce the Ahmadiyya sect of Islam. To obtain a passport or ID card, the following declaration must be made:

> I consider Mirza Ghulam Ahmad an impostor prophet. And also consider his followers, whether belonging to the Lahori or Qadiani group, to be non-Muslims.

Mirza Ghulam Ahmad is worshipped by Ahmadi Muslims, whom they revere as a post-Mohammed prophet. Most Muslims consider this blasphemous, and the persecution of Ahmadis in Pakistan is well-documented; it includes state oppression (they are not even permitted to quote from the Koran) and murder.

141

Finally, punishments in Iran include death by stoning for adultery or hanging for homosexuality.

Saudi Arabia

LIKE ITS NEMESIS IRAN, Saudi is a human rights catastrophe, governed by brutal sharia law. Amputations, stoning, hangings, all feature in its arsenal of state punishments. Like Iran, it kills and tortures its own people and strictly regulates their lives. There is no freedom of speech, no freedom of conscience, no freedom.

Saudi Arabia is a totalitarian absolute monarchy where the king is both head of State and head of government. Decisions are usually made by the king in conjunction with an unelected government and fellow royals. Elections are rare in Saudi and restricted to municipalities. Women were allowed to vote for the first time in municipal elections of 2015.

While Saudi Arabia is a Sunni state, and Iran a Shia state, they have a great deal in common, including spreading terror all over the world.

Saudi Arabia is known to fund extremist and radical mosques globally. Such mosques preach sedition and oppression and anti-Semitism and misogyny, and yet nothing is done to prevent such mosques from sprouting up like mushrooms throughout Western democracies. Islam, once again, is given free rein.

Turkey

PREVIOUSLY RENOWNED FOR ITS secularism (a rarity in the Muslim world), since Recep Tayyip Erdoğan became its president, Turkey has transformed into a state resembling an Islamic one, and it, too, has brought mayhem to other countries, particularly Europe.

Erdoğan has promised a 'war between the crescent and the cross' and has knowingly opened Turkey's borders to allow masses of migrants to illegally enter Europe; all of them Muslim. Following the migrant crisis of 2015, during which more than a million Muslims entered Europe, Germany witnessed the rise of the Alternative für Deutschland political party. The party promised to preserve German culture and stop immigration. Merkel was displeased and sought to rein in the migration and *take credit for it* (having been the one to invite the migration).

The EU then arranged with Turkey to pay them vast amounts (and promise to revisit Turkey's application to join the EU) to keep migrants at bay. Turkey betrayed the bargain in 2019, and opened its border, bringing chaos to its border with Greece – which then descended into a war zone.

Further evidence of its non-democracy include: In what *The New York Times* called 'a political purge of the governing party's critics,' the numbers of journalists in prison began to rise. In January 2020, Erdoğan made his second attempt to provide amnesty to child rapists if they married their victims – an appalling injustice, and one entirely incompatible with democratic civilisation.

These are just some of the countries that the UN intends to build global peace with. The horrors perpetrated by these countries are simply ignored. We live, instead, in a visible lie and we are all expected to pretend the truth is not true. This is the power of Islam. It has convinced the entire Western world that the emperor is fully clothed and punishes those who can see that he isn't. Any problems associated with the religion are described as problems merely attached to a small minority of extremists. This is promoted even though several hugely powerful nations are governed by this very extremism.

The problem with Islam is not a tiny minority of extremists, it is the religion itself. The Koran commands that Muslims use force to subjugate non-Muslims everywhere and all the time. There is nothing in the Koran to suggest that the violence used for spreading Islam is in any way illegitimate – quite the opposite. Here in the West, we are pumped full of lies that have become so familiar, so often repeated, that millions have decided to practice complete cognitive dissonance and believe what they know not to be true. For example, 'Islam means peace.' But those of us who know Islam know that its version of 'peace' is quite different from the rest of the world's understanding. Islam, as a word, has a double meaning; it means both peace and submission. The reason for this is that Islam believes that peace equals submission. In other words, when we all submit to Islam, there will be peace. If we resist, there will not.

'There is no compulsion in religion' is a widely quoted scripture from the Koran; also, it is widely misused, deliberately so, by Western politicians and press to flat-out lie about Islam. There is no compulsion in the sense that Muslims cannot force us to become Muslims, we can instead live as second-class citizens in an Islamic state, but this non-compulsion does not apply to apostates; but we are told that it does. Apostasy carries the death penalty in Islam, but people who know this still willingly believe the 'compulsion' lie. Islam has completely transformed our concept of truth and reality. We, as societies, our politicians, our press, our education, our education system, all insist that Islam is peaceful, despite the barbarism committed in its name all over the world, and despite the barbarism, murder, and hatred contained, wall to wall, in its scriptures. That is the power of Islam.

In Britain, gangs of Muslims have gang-raped white English for decades while the police look away, afraid to confront them. Instead, they persecute those who highlight the rapes and try to bring them to an end. The press does this too, even to Labour (left-wing) MP Sarah Champion, who merely wrote that Pakistani men were raping white girls in her constituency (Rotherham) in a national newspaper. Despite everyone knowing that this statement is 100% true, she was still sacked from her front bench job by the Labour leader and denounced as a racist by many.

Nobody is permitted to cover their faces in various public places in the UK, such as banks, several shops, airports, and courtrooms. There is one exception though – Muslims. Muslims are free to cover their faces with a full niqab, even in airports, and if anyone points out the unfairness of this, they will be accused of racism.

Despite being a criminal offence carrying a hefty 14-year prison sentence, female genital mutilation carries on with impunity in the UK, because it is committed by Muslims.

We are, in effect, living in a state of Islamic supremacy, and the whole world is vying to be as Islamo-friendly as they can. Even sport is vying for Islam's approval. Sporting events, including the Olympics, have thrown long-held clothing rules in the bin to accommodate Islam. Now Muslim women can compete wearing entirely different clothes and can cover their heads with a hijab, as has happened at the Olympic Games. The simpering Islamophiliacs of the media lapped it up and sold it to the public as progress. Women were now 'able to compete' with a hijab. But those women were already able to compete (they just needed to take off their hijab), but this idea is not so much as entertained. The hijab in Islam is worn for female 'modesty.' Logic tells us then that women who don't wear it are immodest. Women's restrictive clothing in Islam is based upon the notion that women cause fitna (chaos) simply by being seen; therefore, in strict Islamic states, women must cover from head to toe. It is also deemed to make a woman 'respectable.' If a woman

147

doesn't wear it and is sexually assaulted, they are to blame. That is what the hijab stands for, and women the world over are murdered, tortured, or imprisoned for taking it off. That's what world sport is happy to promote, and promote it as a good thing, despite the awful truth staring us all in the face.

That is the power of Islam.

Globalism

'GLOBALISM' IS ONE OF those words that everyone knows but few can define. Some argue that the world is no longer politically left or right, but nationalist or globalist: the fight within democracies, then, is for the voters' choice between one or the other.

In Britain, Conservative, Labour, Liberal Democrat, and the SNP (in other words, all the parties in our Parliament), are committed globalists. It's the same across Europe. While nationalist movements are rising, governments are still dominated by those committed to opening the world up to one great, big market.

The problem with globalism is that there is no agreed definition of the word. A little like 'racism,' it is used as an attack word, quite often inappropriately. The term globalisation roughly refers to the interconnectivity of the world; a globalist is one who assumes this to be good and wants more of it. Globalisation is economic or political. 'Globalised trade' means we can buy strawberries all year long; it also means the transfer of jobs from the West to poor countries, and in the process, gutting our own working class and working-class towns.

Its political identity is found in internationalist bodies which, while having little formal political power, set the global tone and lecture national governments on any policy that goes against globalisation. The United Nations and the EU are the two primary examples of globalist governance; the EU, unlike the UN, does have power – lots of it.

As for the global migration included in a globalist viewpoint, this goes in one direction – from the rest of the world to the West. That's the traffic – and it is not by accident.

This is not a conspiracy theory, there is nothing underhand occurring here, it is all happening in plain sight. It is a powerful political philosophy making itself reality.

The world is ruled by an increasingly connected and increasingly wealthy elite; it is ruled – in other words – by big money and big business, and it is they who are calling the shots. Why would big business demand a mass exodus to the West? Simply because the West is too well off, and Westerners demand good pay and good working conditions. People from countries steeped in poverty will simply be glad to have work – any work – which translates to them taking far lower wages and working in much worse conditions. This all saves money for big business. It also decimates the working opportunities of Westerners, keeping wages low and increasing poverty levels along the way.

Western politicians are happy with this for a couple of reasons; 1) they want big business to be pleased with them, 2) they want an increasingly impoverished population. This allows them to reduce the confidence, wealth, and power of their citizens which, in turn, allows them to pass laws restricting our rights. There is no better example of this than 'hate speech.' Hate speech is an old trick of communism, labelling political opposition as wholly immoral (ie, 'hate') and then criminalising that 'hate.' In short, it has criminalised its opposition, allowing it free reign in politics. That reality is evident all over Europe. Oppose open-border migration? You're guilty of 'hate,' and globalist governments are very happy to destroy your life (or imprison you) for having the temerity to swim against the tide and think independently.

Anti-white hatred is also integral to globalism. The West is (still, but only for now) the freest and richest part of the globe. For globalism to work, the West's citizens must be made less free and less wealthy. This is achieved through mass migration from the Third World to the First. In order for the majority in Europe to accept that scenario, that majority must be psychologically defeated, unwilling to fight for its own position – and even its own rights.

To persuade White Europe to hand over its countries to the globalists, whites first must be persuaded that it is what we deserve. As whites, we are inherently evil and the only way to escape this, our only shot at redemption, is to surrender our land, our culture, our heritage, and even our jobs.

Not only did whites allow our borders to be opened, but we've been so self-hating and docile that we even agreed to laws which give non-whites an advantage in the jobs market: 'positive discrimination.' We opened our borders, then bowed down in apology and obedience to those who arrived; all the while destroying our own way of life and our personal prospects.

This is globalism – it is the destruction of the free and wealthy Western populations.

Global trade is the sales pitch. What globalism means economically is a world of buying and selling across borders. In practical terms, it means to deliberately move manufacturing from the rich West to the poor East, leaving the West with broken working-class communities, while the East thrives – and all at much lower cost to the multinationals.

During the coronavirus crisis, it became glaringly evident just how weak globalism had made the West. For supplies of simple protective clothing (PPE) for our medical staff, we turned towards Turkey. We paid our money, the PPE never arrived, we sent our Air Force to collect the PPE, only to find it was substandard and we couldn't use it.

We needed ventilators, but producers in the UK seemed unable to build machines that met with NHS specifications, so we went to China instead. Nine days after the ventilators arrived from China, doctors wrote to the government stating that the machines were more likely to kill patients than save them.

Here we are, a major wealthy First World nation, and we are unable to produce our own basic products for the health of our citizens, even in a time of life-threatening upheaval. Do we need more evidence to demonstrate the downfall of the West, and with it, democracy?

The Far Left

COMMUNISM, SOCIALISM, MARXISM, CALL it what you will, this divisive and destructive philosophy is currently as powerful in the democratic West as it has been in my lifetime. In fact, its power is rapidly expanding, and in 2020, it reached new peaks.

There is no better way to describe the left-wing assault on democracy, no better example to give, than the rise of the far-left terror group Black Lives Matter.

In May 2020, George Floyd, a career criminal with a conviction for the armed robbery of a pregnant woman in her home under his belt, died during an arrest in the US city of Minneapolis. The death was captured on film and occurred when police held Mr Floyd to the ground with force to the back of his neck. Floyd had serious underlying health problems, but his death was attributed to the police; Black Lives Matter (BLM) took to the streets.

The weeks that followed were unprecedented. The entire Western world saw mass protests about Mr Floyd's death, and crucially, demands to rid society of the police altogether.

Black Lives Matter is a communist-anarchist group that seeks to bring down Western democracy and replace it with totalitarianism. They have not hidden this. In addition to de-funding the police, they want to end capitalism, and essentially subject us to a 'society' of chaos and violence. This is what all far-left campaigns seek to do. But Black Lives Matter is different, something odd is occurring here. They have, despite radical and enormously dangerous views, received the support

153

of the entirety of the Western elite establishment. BLM wants to end democracy, and the leaders of democracies are keen to help them.

The protests following Floyd's death have made their intentions clear. Violent thugs have brought fear and destruction to neighbourhoods in the US and UK. You'll often find that when the Western hardleft goes on the rampage; the US and UK are its primary targets. This instance is no different.

In the US, protestors tore down statues of historical figures, many of whom are responsible for the creation of American democracy e.g., the United States' Founding Fathers and authors of its democratic constitution. Black Lives Matter even tore down a statue of Abraham Lincoln – the President responsible for ending slavery in America. It seems odd that they would target Lincoln in the name of 'Black Lives Matter,' just as it is odd to see 'anti-fascists' in the UK demand the removal of a statue of Winston Churchill from central London.

In Britain, BLM attacked our history and heritage, just as it had in the United States. George Orwell wrote in his novel *1984*, how Ingsoc (the new totalitarian leadership of England) had torn down statues and renamed streets in order to demoralize the people and remove their historical sense of unity and purpose. People with no history have no future, and BLM knows this. It is relentlessly attacking Western freedom, to replace it with a kind of communism, and it is meeting little opposition.

The face it puts forward is one primarily concerned with three things: police brutality towards Black people, historical slavery, and 'systemic racism.' In reality, it cares nothing for any of these issues. It is exploiting people's good nature by lying about its intent and pretending they are fighting for racial equality. The truth is far less noble.

Statistics confirm that Blacks are not specifically subject to police brutality in the United States. America can be a violent place, guns are widely owned, and armed police are frequently confronted with the possibility of extreme violence. Statistics show however, that year on year, more white people are killed by police in the United States than Black people. BLM's primary selling point, then, is a lie.

That's not the only lie. Slavery is obviously abhorrent; it was yesterday, and it is today. Slavery is still alive and well today in Africa for example, but BLM says nothing about it. This is despite the fact that it is usually Black people who are being sold into slavery even as I write. The problem for BLM is that these Black people are sold into slavery by other Black people, therefore there is silence. BLM however has decided that the US and the UK, both of whom were instrumental in ending slavery in the West, are to be targeted, but not the African countries selling slaves in 2020. Isn't this strange? Not when you know that Black Lives Matter is lying. It cares nothing for slavery, its attack is against capitalism – but even more so, democracy.

The final lie propped up by the press and politicians on behalf of BLM is that they seek racial equality. The problem is, we've already got racial equality. Let me correct myself: we don't have racial equality; whites do not have the same opportunities as Blacks in the UK. In many job advertisements, whites are excluded from applying; thus, white people are legally discriminated against in the UK. If BLM were concerned about equality, wouldn't they object to this?

You get the picture. BLM is a communist sham and front group whose sole purpose is to create a broken society, raze the West to the ground, and rule over the rubble. They showed us the kind of society they want to build and what's in store when they took over a small area of the city of Seattle and proceeded to build their utopia inside.

The first thing they did in their new Capitol Hill Autonomous Zone (CHAZ) was to build a border around it. BLM wants open borders across the globe but wants to protect its own area with a wall. This should surprise nobody.

They drove the police out of the area and then wondered why nobody came to help them when they needed it. Someone had been hurt inside, according to social media posts at the time, and died while waiting for help. But they had rejected help by excluding the police. The blame, of course, went to the police.

When violence is an issue, paramedics will not see to patients unless the police have first secured the area. Police are not allowed in CHAZ, so paramedics won't attend. BLM participants are learning – as if they are small children – that society needs structure, and the systems we've put in place are actually quite successful. This is a lesson they are learning fast.

With no police, theft is commonplace inside the utopia. People walk around casually with heavy-duty guns and there have been, at the time of writing, at least two shootings inside. With no capitalist food supply, they were forced to beg for sustenance on Twitter. What an absolute fiasco, and anyone with a morsel of intelligence could have seen it coming – theft, violence, destruction – but not BLM.

Now, given all of this, wouldn't you expect Western governments to be handling this firmly and fairly? Not happening. Western governments, and major politicians, the state, the police, journalists – even the NFL – are literally down on their knees prostrating themselves to BLM. It is one of the starkest displays of the imminent peril facing our civilized societies.

In London, BLM thugs tried to pull down the central London statue of Sir Winston Churchill. There are several statues of Churchill in the UK, but this is the one that adorns Parliament Square – the beautiful central London location of the Houses of Parliament. Churchill's statue is large and dominates the square, looking proudly across at the Parliament in which he once sat as Prime Minister. He is, undoubtedly, one of the most revered figures in all British history. His legacy? Standing alone in Europe against Adolf Hitler and fighting to bring fascism on the continent to an end. Churchill fought fascism tooth and nail, but his statue is threatened by people who call themselves 'anti-fascist.'

While the thugs did not manage to tear down the Churchill statue, they did deface it with smears of 'racist' graffitied on to its plinth. While this criminal offence was committed, the British police stood and watched. They did nothing. Instead of arresting and prosecuting people who had committed a crime while the country watched, the political and policing establishment gave them their wish. The central London statue of Winston Churchill is, as I write, covered from head to toe in a huge metal box. We have made Churchill invisible at the behest of a violent anti-democratic group of anarchists.

Prime Minister Boris Johnson did nothing about this either. Churchill's statue is only a short walk from 10 Downing Street (the Prime Minister's residence) and yet, there it stands, cold and covered, while our 'conservative' Prime Minister has little to say except to sanitise the group and pretend it has been hijacked by bad apples. It has not. It is a bad apple, and its extreme ideas are the foundation of its cause.

The following week, when British patriots (including myself), veterans, and concerned citizens gathered to protect the Churchill statue, we were denounced as racist thugs by Johnson and others in his cabinet.

If you know Britain, you'll know how calamitous this is; Churchill replaced in the pecking order by arch-communist anarchists.

So important are these anarchists, and so obeyed, that even England's world-famous Premier League has agreed to submit. The Premier League is England's premier football tournament ('soccer' to our American friends) and is without doubt the most popular sporting event in the country each year. In 2020, while playing to empty stadiums – thanks to coronavirus – players were obliged to 'take a knee' in honour of an American career criminal and the liars exploiting his death to install communism. Yes, UK footballers, most of them multimillionaires, got on their knees to communism. It is as clear as night follows day that many of them don't understand what they are actually 'taking a knee' for. That's the genius of Black Lives Matter. They've dressed themselves up in such moral finery that if you object, you automatically become the worst of the worst. Who will object to the idea that Black lives matter? Of course, they do, but BLM couldn't care less about Black lives. It would be interesting to hear what the millionaire footballers think about handing over all their wealth and property for collective use.

Television, newspapers, schools, all of them are promoting Black Lives Matter in the UK. But perhaps the most nauseating scene of all, just as disturbing as seeing Churchill made invisible in London, was watching London's old and respected Metropolitan Police 'take a knee' in response to demands from BLM thugs. Police actually got on to their knees in obedience to a far-left radical communist anarchist violent political organisation.

As they say, *let that sink in.*

All of this could make us despair, it could cause us to slink away and forget it all; many already believe saving Western democracy is a lost cause. But that is the hope of BLM and other dangerous groups – to let us believe they have won, but they have not. Despite the media's best efforts to persuade us otherwise, democrats are the majority, and we retain all the strength and determination of the democrats that went before us, and we will do what they did.

Throughout history, men and women struggled (and died) for democracy. Our past is littered with battles between freedom and tyranny. History has not stopped, we are living it now, and if the future is to have democracy, we will have to do just what our ancestors did – *fight.*

Conclusion

HISTORY REPEATS. IT'S A phrase that is difficult to argue with because it's true. The history of the Western world is proof.

In Europe, for all recorded history, we have drifted from notions of democracy and self-rule (from the times of ancient Greece), and when established, it was established through bloodshed. Democracy did not just spring into being; it is the result of centuries of fragile humanity trying to find a way to organise itself in a way that was best for most. We tried to find ways to increase the prospects and opportunity for the poorest to ensure that no one individual could determine the fate of millions. Democracy was the answer we arrived at. Here in Europe, we have had democracy for some decades now, but the tide of history is, once again, turning. The same war for liberty must be fought today as it was yesterday and the day before that.

This is a different kind of war. Today, we are not required to die in trenches as brave men did in the past. We are not going to fly over Germany and drop bombs or annihilate cities. Instead, our war is one of information and truth.

Western democracies are not threatened by force, but by lies and propaganda. Patriots are described as 'racist,' democrats as 'fascists,' secularists as 'hate-mongers,' and peaceful protestors as 'thugs.' The opposite is the truth, yet our media maintains the false narrative, meaning that weak politicians do, as well. Like Donald Trump, only strong politicians will defy the press and act in the interests of democracy. That is the leadership the West needs but is sorely lacking.

159

CONCLUSION

Despite the lies, hatred, and the racial division deliberately stoked up by the hard-left, the democratic remain the majority; the problem is that they no longer realise it. The media and ruling class have persuaded the common-sense majority that there is something wrong with them. There is not.

The same media will lie to cover up for – and accommodate – the communist nightmare that is China. China is led by a dark, sinister, and cruel cabal. It is rapidly becoming the world's leading country and will happily reduce the United States to a mere shadow of its former self. Ironically, it will do so with the help of America's elite.

Globalism is on the march, and big business wants cheap labour imported to the West to keep its costs down. This depresses wages in the West or sends manufacturing overseas altogether at the expense of countless jobs. The Western working class has been decimated and destroyed by globalism, and democracy will be its primary victim.

Finally, there is Islam. A violent and ferociously undemocratic religion has been imported into Western countries and allowed absolute freedom to break our laws and supplant our culture. Islam has brought murder and mayhem to our streets, undermined women, threatened Jews and homosexuals, and all but wiped out our vital and historical right to criticize power – including religious power.

All of this is happening because the media continues to lie, and the politicians continue to bow down to the lies. Therefore, to save our democracies, we must counter the lies and promote the truth at any cost.

We live in the internet age; therefore, we have options. We can produce our own media reports, we can promote evidence, stand up and tell it like it is – it's what our people are desperate for. We must remember our power and take hold of it. (Politicians are only in power because we put them there.) We must stop.

The most important thing we can do, however, is stand for election *and win*. This is our way out. The press will make this as difficult as possible, but it has overplayed its hand. So many lies have been told by the media now that its credibility among the public has spiralled.

This is our chance.

IN DEFENSE OF DEMOCRACY

Let us get up from our knees and talk to people. Let us knock on doors, print our leaflets, make our websites, and hold our public meetings. There is nothing the press can do to stop it. Unless they plan to ban elections, there is nothing the political elite can do about it either.

We must bypass the corrupted system of 2020 and bring politics straight back to the high street, pubs, clubs, societies, and the church halls...we must wear out our shoes and never – *ever* – give up.

We must use the only thing still freely available to us – our vote. We must, in other words, use our democracy *to save* our democracy.

www.ingramcontent.com/pod-product-compliance
Lightning Source LLC
Chambersburg PA
CBHW072250270326
41930CB00010B/2334